SO-AFY-983

New Directions for
Higher Education

Betsy O. Barefoot
Jillian L. Kinzie
CO-EDITORS

# College Completion for Latino/a Students: Institutional and System Approaches

Melissa L. Freeman
Magdalena Martinez

EDITORS

Number 172 • Winter 2015
Jossey-Bass
San Francisco

Americans. By 2060 Latino/as are projected to represent 31% of the total U.S. population (Santiago, Calderón Galdeano, & Taylor, 2015).

This growth implies a shift in the demographic makeup of the U.S. labor force. According to the Bureau of Labor Statistics (Toossi, 2012), Latino/as will constitute almost 20% of the U.S. labor force by 2020, with 65% of all jobs requiring some form of postsecondary education or training. With a projected 55 million job openings by 2020, should the current completion rate remain the same, the United States will be short about 5 million workers who have the postsecondary education necessary to perform those jobs (Carnevale & Strohl, 2013).

Despite some recent gains in postsecondary enrollment, the educational pipeline still continues to hemorrhage Latino/as. Although Latino/as account for 24% of the nation's elementary and secondary school enrollment, they represent only 19% and 11% of the nation's community college and 4-year institution enrollments, respectively (Excelencia in Education, 2015; Hispanic Association of Colleges and Universities, 2015; Snyder & Dillow, 2012). And, most Latino/as attend Hispanic-serving institutions (HSIs), which account for 12.1% of all nonprofit colleges/universities in the United States. HSIs enroll 20% of all students, but nearly two-thirds (58.9%) of all Latino/a students attend HSIs exclusively, up significantly in the last several years (Hispanic Association of Colleges and Universities, 2015; Santiago, 2006).

## Hispanic-Serving Institutions

Hispanic-serving institutions are defined as "accredited and degree-granting public or private nonprofit institutions of higher education with 25% or more total undergraduate Hispanic full-time equivalent student enrollment" (Santiago, 2006, p. 5). By their very definition, HSIs were developed as a response to large concentrations of Latino/a students in institutions of higher education (IHEs) and not as institutional mandates to *serve* Latino/a students. As such, Hispanic-serving institutions have historically been "characterized by their enrollment ratios rather than by their institutional mission" (Santiago, 2006, p. 5).

It was not until the early 1980s that institutional leaders began to raise national awareness about growing Latino/a enrollments on their campuses. The first mention of "Hispanic institutions" occurred in 1983 during Congressional hearings that focused on Latino/a access to higher education. In these hearings it was noted that (a) Latino/as lacked access and were not successful in completion and (b) Latino/as attended institutions with limited financial support, which hampered the ability to improve their success. In response, Congressman Paul Simon (D-IL) introduced legislation to provide support to institutions that served large numbers of Latino/a students at "Hispanic institutions." Meanwhile, a group of institutional leaders and other interested parties founded the Hispanic Association of Colleges and

Universities (HACU) to raise recognition of and investment in those institutions and others with student enrollments that were at least 25% Hispanic. At HACU's inaugural meeting in 1986, members coined the phrase "Hispanic-serving institution." Despite this growing attention, it was not until 1992 that federal legislation officially recognized HSIs through Title III of the Higher Education Act. It would take 3 more years for federal funding to be allocated. Thus, in 1995, 37 of the 189 existing HSIs received $12 million in federal appropriations under Title V's Developing HSIs Program. Funding has continued over the years; as recently as 2013, 151 of 370 HSIs received approximately $95 million in program support (Santiago, 2006; Villarreal & Santiago, 2012). However, two issues are important to note. First, the federal designation and financial support differ significantly for HSIs versus minority-serving institutions (MSIs), historically Black colleges and universities (HBCUs), or tribal colleges and universities (TCUs). Title V funding is not mandated nor guaranteed for all HSIs. Rather, HSIs must meet stringent criteria as outlined by the federal government to qualify *to apply for* competitive grants "because it was not based on a compensatory rationale, but instead a demographic increase and shift" (Gasman, Nguyen, & Conrad, 2014, p. 9). Second, although the most recent appropriation of $95 million may seem like a significant increase from the original $12 million, Title V funds have been substantially cut in recent years. This, coupled with the increasing number of HSIs, means fewer dollars are available to increased numbers of institutions and students (Maldonaldo, 2015). To date, the number of HSIs has increased to 409, up more than 30 institutions in just 1 year (Santiago, 2015). Nearly one half (190) are 2-year institutions, and another one quarter (81) represent public 4-year institutions. Overall, these institutions enroll more than 2.9 million Latino/as in the United States and Puerto Rico (Hispanic Association of Colleges and Universities, 2015).

## Volume Overview

Research about ways institutions are working to best serve Latino/a students is limited. Yet, national and institutional leaders must have an understanding of what works to ensure effective policy for Latino/a student success. The purpose of this volume is to fill the gap about Latino/a student success by exploring institutional- or system-level approaches. This volume explores how institutions are working to meet the demands of the growing population of Latino/a students. Chapter 1 is a case study of the Higher Education Administration & Leadership (HEAL) program at Adams State University, which focuses on "Preparing the Next Generation of Leaders at the Nation's Hispanic-Serving Institutions." Freeman provides important insights for institutions interested in creating leadership programs or pathways for professionals at HSIs. Chapter 2 examines organizational change through a group of emerging HSIs and their governance, policy, and

NEW DIRECTIONS FOR HIGHER EDUCATION • DOI: 10.1002/he

leadership. Martinez highlights the challenges and opportunities for emerging HSIs and lessons learned from one specific state, Nevada. In Chapter 3, Kiyama, Museus, and Vega highlight the factors that hinder or contribute to the success of Latino/a students at predominantly White institutions. The Culturally Engaging Campus Environments (CECE) Model is used as a framework to create environments in which all students can thrive in college. Chapter 4 focuses on the institutionalization of support for undocumented students across states. Gildersleeve and Vigil highlight promising practices for states and institutions.

Chapter 5 offers a mixed-methods study of personal and programmatic factors that affected persistence of Latina graduate engineering students at an HSI. Aguirre-Covarrubias, Arellano, and Espinoza provide findings and recommendations useful to HSIs and other colleges and universities interested in expanding success of Latina STEM (science, technology, engineering, mathematics) students. Chapter 6 examines Latino male ethnic subgroups and their college enrollment and degree completion patterns. Ponjuan, Palomin, and Calise offer recommendations to improve their educational achievement. González, in Chapter 7, discusses ways in which leadership in community colleges can increase Latino/a student success through effective strategies.

Chapter 8 shifts the focus to the role of financial aid and HSIs. Venegas synthesizes literature related to postsecondary institutions with large Hispanic populations and their financial aid practices. She offers a framework for guiding institutions interested in aligning their financial aid practices with Latino student success. In Chapter 9, Natividad examines the importance of culturally relevant imagery and representation and identity development curriculum for college students. He calls for higher education institutions to embrace cultural strengths as an asset rather than a deficit. In Chapter 10, Saladino and Martinez offer a synthesis of recommendations to aid academics and practitioners as they develop policy and practice to support Latino/a students.

As a collective, the chapters in this volume encompass topics such as Latino/a undergraduate student success, graduate student success, community colleges, 4-year institutions, financial aid, and undocumented students. Through original research, literature reviews, and case studies, this volume highlights best practices and successful initiatives and outcomes for Latino/a students. We draw attention to what works, and specifically, how institutions can best serve Latino/as from matriculation to graduation given their unique needs. As such, institutions of higher education can truly become Hispanic *serving*.

Melissa L. Freeman
Magdalena Martinez
Editors

# References

Carnevale, A. P., & Strohl, J. (2013). *Separate & equal: How higher education reinforces intergenerational reproduction of white racial privilege.* Retrieved from https://cew.georgetown.edu/wp-content/uploads/2014/11/SeparateUnequal.FR_.pdf

Excelencia in Education. (2015). *Hispanic-serving institutions: Title V funding timeline.* Washington, DC: Author. Retrieved from http://www.edexcelencia.org/hsi-cp2/hsis-101/hsi-timelines/funding-timeline

Gasman, M., Nguyen, T., & Conrad, C. F. (2014). Lives intertwined: A primer on the history and emergence of minority serving institutions. *Journal of Diversity in Higher Education.* Advance online publication. doi:10.1037/a0038386

Hispanic Association of Colleges and Universities. (2015). *Fact sheet: Hispanic higher education and HSIs 2015.* Retrieved from http://www.hacu.net/hacu/HSI_Fact_Sheet.asp

Maldonaldo, L. (2015, March 9). Plenary address. Seventh Annual HSI/Title V Best Practices Conference, Association of Hispanic Serving Institution Educators (AHSIE), San Antonio, TX.

Russell, A. (2011). *A guide to major U.S. college completion initiatives.* Washington, DC: American Association of State Colleges and Universities. Retrieved from http://www.aascu.org/policy/publications/policymatters/2011/collegecompletion.pdf

Santiago, D. A. (2006). *Inventing Hispanic-serving institutions (HSIs): The basics.* Washington, DC: Excelencia in Education. Retrieved from http://www.edexcelencia.org/hsi-cp2/research/inventing-hispanic-serving-institutions-basics

Santiago, D. A. (2015, March 10). Plenary address. Seventh Annual HSI/Title V Best Practices Conference, Association of Hispanic Serving Institution Educators (AHSIE), San Antonio, TX.

Santiago, D. A., Calderón Galdeano, E., & Taylor, M. (2015). *The condition of Latinos in education: 2015 factbook.* Washington, DC: Excelencia in Education. Retrieved from http://www.edexcelencia.org/research/2015-factbook

Santiago, D. A., & Callan, P. (2010). *Ensuring America's future: Benchmarking Latino college completion to meet national goals: 2010 to 2020.* Washington, DC: Excelencia in Education. Retrieved from http://www.edexcelencia.org/research/benchmarking-latino-college-completion

Snyder, T. D., & Dillow, S. A. (2012). *Digest of education statistics 2013* (NCES 2014-015). Washington, DC: U.S. Department of Education, National Center for Education Statistics.

Toossi, M. (2012). *Labor force projections to 2020: A more slowly growing workforce.* Retrieved from http://www.bls.gov/opub/mlr/2012/01/art3full.pdf

White House, Office of the Press Secretary. (2009, February 24). *Remarks of President Barack Obama—as prepared for delivery: Address to joint session of Congress.* Retrieved from http://www.whitehouse.gov/the-press-office/remarks-president-barack-obama-address-joint-session-congress

Villarreal, R. C., & Santiago, D. A. (2012). *From capacity to success: HSIs and Latino student success through Title V.* Washington, DC: Excelencia in Education.

MELISSA L. FREEMAN *is the founding director of the Higher Education Administration and Leadership (HEAL) program at Adams State University. She is currently the director of the Center for Graduate Studies and the activity director of the Title V PPOHA grant at Adams State.*

MAGDALENA MARTINEZ *is the director of education programs at the Lincy Institute and a faculty member in the College of Education at the University of Nevada, Las Vegas.*

NEW DIRECTIONS FOR HIGHER EDUCATION • DOI: 10.1002/he

1

*This chapter is a case study of the Higher Education Administration and Leadership (HEAL) program at Adams State University. HEAL focuses on preparing the next generation of leaders at the nation's Hispanic-serving institutions.*

# HEALing Higher Education: An Innovative Approach to Preparing HSI Leaders

*Melissa L. Freeman*

"Why is the leadership at this Hispanic-serving institution all White males?" (A. Salazar, Adams State University Board of Trustees member, personal communication, 2008). Trustee Salazar articulated a specific example of what many had predicted would occur in higher education without a strategic and deliberate leadership pipeline plan: a Latino/a higher education leadership crisis. The number of Latino/a students enrolled in the nation's colleges and universities is increasing rapidly, but the number of students who are rising to leadership positions is not keeping pace. As shown in Table 1.1, 24% of all students in the nation's elementary and secondary schools are Latinos/as, yet Latino/as represent only 19% of 2-year college students and 11% of 4-year college students. Equally troubling is that Latinos represent only 5% of institutional administrators and less than 4% of faculty.

This mismatch between the backgrounds of the students and their educational leaders can be corrected only by increasing the number of Latino/as in leadership positions. As Betts, Urias, Chavez, and Betts (2009) describe the situation,

> To increase diversity in higher education administration, institutions must begin by recruiting increased numbers of minorities to work within colleges and universities ... It is through increasing diversity in the leadership pipeline and through professional development that diversity will become more reflective on all levels of administration; ultimately becoming even more reflective within senior administration and the presidency. (p. 5)

Too few Latino/a students are entering graduate school and earning the credentials necessary to assume leadership positions in U.S. colleges and

NEW DIRECTIONS FOR HIGHER EDUCATION, no. 172, Winter 2015 © 2015 Wiley Periodicals, Inc.
Published online in Wiley Online Library (wileyonlinelibrary.com) • DOI: 10.1002/he.20148

**Table 1.1. Percentage of Total Enrollment and Employees in U.S. Higher Education System Who Are Hispanic**

| Role | Percent Hispanic |
|------|------------------|
| Elementary/Secondary Schools | 24 |
| Community Colleges | 19 |
| Four-Year Colleges/Universities | 11 |
| Graduate Programs | 8 |
| Senior/Executive/Administrators | 5 |
| Faculty | 4 |

Source: Snyder & Dillow (2012).

universities. For example, in 2006–07, institutions in Colorado awarded 11,672 master's degrees with only 597 (5.1%) awarded to Latino/as. One of the state's two Hispanic-serving institutions (HSIs)—Adams State University (ASU)—has a significantly better record. In 2007–08, ASU awarded 225 master's degrees with 23% of them going to Latino/as. To have a significant impact on the shortage of Latino/a leaders, institutions must significantly increase the numbers of Latino/a students earning master's and doctoral degrees. Congressman Ruben Hinojosa (2004) argued, "It is time to look for ways to seed the pipeline at the advanced degree level where the acute Latino/a underrepresentation threatens to retard growth in other areas such as teaching, health, research, and economic development" (p. 77). Adams State's plan to seed that pipeline is the focus of this chapter.

There are multiple reasons why few Latino/a students enter graduate school (Fry, 2002). Researchers find there is a common experience shared by many Latino/a undergraduates. Many leave college with significant debt, have lower earnings prospects, and have major family responsibilities. These factors often demand that Latinos/as enter the workforce immediately after earning a 4-year degree and wait to begin graduate school later in their careers.

Once new graduates begin working in higher education, virtually all paths to leadership require an advanced degree. Increasing the number of Latino/as with the appropriate credentials to move into leadership requires institutions to design programs offering high-quality, affordable professional development accessible to students who work full time.

The shortage of Latino/a leaders in the nation's HSIs is exacerbated when one considers that, although these institutions represent only 11% of higher education institutions in the United States, they enroll almost 60% of the nation's Latino/a undergraduates. The number of HSIs continues to grow. Excelencia in Education has identified 277 colleges and universities termed "emerging HSIs" or institutions with Hispanic enrollments of 15% to 24.9% (Galdeano & Santiago, 2014). More than 647 U.S. institutions have Latino/a enrollments of more than 15%. HSIs and emerging HSIs must graduate significantly more students, especially Latinos/as. Yet these institutions have a difficult time hiring, developing, and retaining qualified Latino/as into mid- and senior-level positions.

Little attention has been devoted to addressing this leadership gap. HSIs and their faculty/staff have been left to their own devices to find comprehensive leadership development opportunities. Prior to 2010, apart from a 1-day institute offered by the Hispanic Association of Colleges and Universities (HACU), there was no degree or certificate program in higher education leadership designed to serve the needs of HSI leaders. Indeed, of all of the nation's HSIs, only two of them, City University of New York and Texas A&M University–Kingsville, offer master's degrees in higher education leadership, administration, or student affairs. Both are traditional programs that require students to attend face-to-face classes and likely pause their higher education career. In an effort to address this leadership gap, ASU decided to find a way to develop its own online higher education leadership program.

## A Case Study: Adams State University and the Higher Education Administration and Leadership (HEAL) Program

Founded in 1921 as a teachers' college, Adams State University is a small, residential campus located in southern Colorado. As the regional higher education provider, ASU enhances the area's educational opportunity, economic development, and cultural enrichment. The institution has a rich history of serving disenfranchised populations, including underrepresented minorities, first-generation students, and low-income students (Adams State University, 2014a).

In 2000, ASU was the first Colorado higher education institution to be federally designated as an HSI (L. Gomez, personal communication, March 2013). Since then, the university has developed numerous exemplary programs through Title V, TRIO, and other sources of U.S. Department of Education funding that focus on undergraduate Latino/a student success. However, prior to the HEAL program, ASU had not focused on the HSI mission at the graduate level.

In 2008, Arnold Salazar—an ASU alumnus and executive director of the Colorado Health Partnerships, L.L.C.—received a gubernatorial appointment to the ASU Board of Trustees. In his first meeting, he asked the pointed question that opened this chapter, "Why is the leadership at this Hispanic-serving institution all White males?" (A. Salazar, personal communication, March 2014). Provost Michael Mumper sought an answer. After researching dozens of position descriptions and individuals' qualifications, he found many individuals on campus who had the talent to move into leadership positions. However, *they lacked the necessary skill set and credential* to do so—a master's degree.

Unfortunately, this is a problem that many people of color—especially Latino/as—face in higher education. Table 1.1 shows the number of Latino/as in the higher education pipeline drops significantly at each step

(Snyder & Dillow, 2012). This problem is not limited to just the upper echelons of higher education; rather, it is a problem that is endemic throughout the educational pipeline.

**An Initial Plan.**    To address this gap, in 2008, Provost Mumper developed a higher education leadership emphasis in the master's of business administration (MBA) program. Although this was not an ideal option for higher education professionals, it was a first attempt to address the Latino/a leadership shortage. Unfortunately, these programs, even when coupled with existing programs, are expensive to design and implement. Despite ASU's good intentions the university budget collapsed in 2009 and the plan was shelved.

**A New Opportunity.**    In July 2009, the U.S. Department of Education's Fund for the Improvement of Postsecondary Education (FIPSE) program issued a Request for Proposals (RFP) that emphasized "graduate education" and "institutions that serve large numbers of Latinos." At a meeting with Provost Mumper, he asked me three key questions: What would it take to develop a master's degree in higher education? What would it take to develop a master's degree in higher education that focuses on preparing the next generation of leaders in the nation's HSIs? Would I be willing to take the lead in program development?

Under my and Provost Mumper's leadership, ASU then submitted a FIPSE grant proposal, titled "Preparing the Next Generation of Leaders in the Nation's Hispanic-Serving Institutions (HSIs)," to the U.S. Department of Education. The university was awarded this grant, which provided the seed money to develop the Higher Education Administration and Leadership (HEAL) program. This innovative program was designed to prepare early and midcareer professionals to be successful in leadership positions at HSIs. Simply, the HEAL program is about creating *access* to high-quality graduate programs for HSI professionals and increasing Latino/a leadership.

**HEAL Program Development and Approval.**    A FIPSE award did not guarantee that a program would be put into place. After ASU received the award, several additional steps were taken that led to program approval by the state of Colorado. The most salient of these steps was the convening of a curriculum committee responsible for program mission, curriculum, and assessment development. Other than me, the university had no faculty with PhDs in higher education who could develop a program. Thus, we relied on external expertise of both academics and practitioners.

Members of the curriculum committee included faculty and university leaders from both 2- and 4-year institutions as well as the grant-evaluation consultants. All brought to the table a vast array of experiences and knowledge including, but not limited to, recruitment, retention, professional needs of institutions, and higher education curricula. They developed all components of the program including an innovative curriculum, recruitment strategies, practicum and management, e-portfolio/capstone experience, mission statement, learning outcomes, degree plan, course learning

2

*There is limited research on how postsecondary institutions prepare to become HSIs. This chapter examines organizational change through a group of emerging HSIs and their governance, policy, and leadership.*

# An Examination of Organizational Change Through Nevada's Emerging Hispanic-Serving Institutions

*Magdalena Martinez*

It is important to understand organizational change in higher education for at least three reasons: (a) our postmodern times require postsecondary institutions to change in order to respond to a more fragmented and complex environment, (b) the new normal of limited resources and increased public accountability requires institutions to examine multiple ways of being successful, and (c) postsecondary institutions are increasingly less homogenous and need to become more responsive to the multiplicity of various constituents (Kezar, 2001). The purpose of this chapter is to examine how three emerging Hispanic-serving institutions (HSIs) in Nevada and their state higher education agency dealt with organization change in response to the explosive growth of Hispanic[1] undergraduates. Specifically, I use case study methods to understand the role that governance, policy, and leadership played during critical formative years—2009 to 2014. The question that shaped this inquiry was: What are the governance, policy, and leadership issues critical to creating awareness and action toward HSI designation? I situate this analysis in the organizational theories of change, specifically as categorized by Kezar. The lessons learned in this chapter can be informative to other states experiencing significant growth of emerging HSIs.

## Why Focus on Emerging Hispanic-Serving Institutions?

As the name implies, HSIs serve large Hispanic populations, those that are at least 25% Hispanic. Yet when compared to other minority-serving institutions, such as historically Black and tribal colleges and universities, HSIs emerged under different contexts and circumstances. Rather than

NEW DIRECTIONS FOR HIGHER EDUCATION, no. 172, Winter 2015 © 2015 Wiley Periodicals, Inc.
Published online in Wiley Online Library (wileyonlinelibrary.com) • DOI: 10.1002/he.20149

19

being mission driven to serve a specific student population, HSIs are often described as having closeted identities with little intentionality in serving Hispanic students (Contreas, Malcom, & Bensimon, 2008). Postsecondary institutions considered emerging HSIs are those with a Hispanic student population between 15% and 24.9%. As of 2013 there were 370 postsecondary institutions that met the federal enrollment criterion for HSI status and an additional 277 classified as emerging HSIs (Santiago, Galdeano, & Taylor, 2015). The evolution of HSIs is distinct, and they represent the largest group of minority-serving institutions.

Twenty years ago, postsecondary leaders may have argued there was limited scholarship on HSIs and organizational change to help these institutions understand and identify organizational strategies. However recent research on HSIs and Hispanic students as well as examples of successful HSIs (Gasman, 2008; León, 2003; Nuñez, Hurtado, & Galdeano, 2015; Santiago & Andrade, 2010) provides today's institutional leaders ample evidence on how they can prepare, create, and implement successful organizational structures to serve large numbers of Hispanic students. Given their continued growth and the number of students they serve, HSIs have been at the center of the college completion dialogue.

National higher education organizations and researchers argue that the United States will not be the world leader in higher education attainment without an intentional focus on Hispanic undergraduate completion (Santiago & Galdeano, 2015; Vuong & Hairston, 2012). Further, HSIs account for 11% of all postsecondary institutions and educate close to 60% of all Hispanic students nationwide (Santiago, Galdeano, & Taylor, 2015). There has been a recent interest in the role of HSIs, in particular as it relates to the use of data for student success, teaching, curriculum, and student interventions. For instance, in Chapter 7 in this volume Gonzalez examines the role of data, national initiatives for HSIs, and some of the successes and limitations of big data initiatives and implications for HSIs. Aguirre-Covarrubias, Arellano, and Espinoza in Chapter 5, Natividad in Chapter 9, and Freeman in Chapter 1 focus on the role of institutional culture and its effect on student engagement and success.

A focus on interventions is warranted; however, researchers also need to understand the role of governance, policy, and leadership at existing HSIs and in particular at those institutions on the cusp of becoming HSIs. It is important to understand how postsecondary institutions behave, respond, and approach their emerging HSI status, and organizationally, what changes, pressures, or adjustments are needed as the institutions interface with multiple actors and external organizations.

## Organizational Theories of Change

Kezar (2001) places organizational theories of change into six categories. According to Kezar, each theory is meant to help in understanding, describing, and developing insights about the change process and includes a set of assumptions about why change occurs, how the process unfolds, when change occurs and how long it takes, and the outcomes of change. For instance, evolutionary theories assume that change is a response to external circumstances and the environment faced by each organization. Teleological theories or rational models assume that organizations are purposeful and adaptive and change occurs because members—whether leaders, change agents, or others—see the necessity of change. The process of change is rational and linear as it is in evolutionary change models. Life cycle theories focus on organizational growth or decline, and change is seen as a natural part of organizational development. Political models see change as a result of clashing ideology or belief systems, and conflict is viewed as an inherent attribute of interactions. Social cognition models refer to the connection of change to sense making and mental models. Change occurs because people recognize a need to grow, learn, and change their behavior. In cultural models, change occurs naturally as a response to alterations in the human environment; the change process usually is long term and slow and entails the alteration of values, beliefs, myths, and rituals.

Kezar (2001) suggests that although one theory cannot entirely explain organizational change, a combination of these can help researchers achieve greater clarity and an understanding of the complexities of organizations and the individuals that occupy them. Further, she suggests that higher education institutions seem to be best interpreted through cultural, social-cognition, and political models.

## The Explosive Hispanic Growth in Nevada

To say the Hispanic population in Nevada has experienced a significant growth is an understatement. From 1990 to 2000 there was a 264% change in Hispanic population, one of the largest across any demographic group in the state. In 2011, Nevada ranked 14th in the nation in numbers of Latino/as (Pew Research Center, 2011). In the same year, Latino/as comprised 27% of the total state population with more than half native born. The majority were of Mexican origin, and overall, Hispanics were much younger with a median age of 26, compared to 38 for non-Hispanic Whites.

Not surprisingly, the Latino/a population growth in Nevada was particularly acute in the kindergarten through 12th grade (K–12) levels. Latino/a students accounted for more than 40% of the K–12 enrollment (Nevada Legislative Counsel Bureau, 2013a). Yet the enrollment did not translate to high school graduation and college enrollment. For instance, the high school adjusted cohort graduation rate for Latino/as for 2011 was 60% compared to 78% for Whites, and college enrollment rates immediately after high school for Fall 2011 were 56% compared to 65% for Whites (Nevada Department of Education, n.d.). Despite the low high school and college graduation rates in the state, Nevada is one of only six states in which Latino/a undergraduate enrollment accounts for at least 20% of all undergraduate enrollment (Santiago, Galdeano, & Taylor, 2015).

The situation is further complicated because during the Great Recession of 2007 through 2009, Nevada suffered one of the most precipitous budget decreases compared to any other state in the nation. In a *Chronicle of Higher Education* article on state cuts to public higher education, Hebel (2010) summarizes it as follows:

> No one factor can indicate which states and their college systems are in the most serious trouble. But in no states do prospects look bleaker for public higher education than in Nevada, where fiscal, demographic, and academic challenges all rank among the toughest in the nation.
>
> The state's projected budget gap for next year is the country's largest, measured by the proportion of general-fund budget, a shortfall expected to equal nearly 60% of Nevada's total budget. Over the next 10 years, the number of high-school graduates in the state is expected to grow by 26%, the fastest rise in the United States. And Nevada already struggles with college-pipeline problems, ranking 50th among the states on the likelihood of its ninth graders to earn a high-school diploma, with only about 56% doing so. (para. 9–10)

It was precisely during the same period that Nevada's public postsecondary institutions were becoming emerging HSIs.

## Nevada's Emerging Hispanic-Serving Institutions and the Great Recession

In 2012–13, there were 277 new emerging HSIs across 16 states. In the state of Nevada all seven public college and universities were emerging HSIs. Santiago (2009) reminds us that the poorly kept secret in higher education is that these institutions will eventually meet the enrollment criteria to be identified as HSIs but their leaders cannot articulate what it means to "serve" Latino/a students. The same can be said for emerging HSIs. These institutions have the opportunity to be deliberate about their emerging status.

Like many states, Nevada has raised its tuition and fees to make up the gap of state support to public higher education ("Higher ed reality," 2011; Myers, 2011). During the 76th Nevada State Legislature, policymakers also approved a study to revamp higher education funding that moved it from a formula- to an outcome-based model (Nevada Legislative Counsel Bureau, 2013b). At the same time, the state's citizen legislature members saw the opportunity for public postsecondary institutions to apply for federal grants—such as HSI Title V grants—to make up some of the budget

Finally, an understanding of organizational change theories can help ease the transition and tension points institutions will experience as they become HSIs. Change is inevitable in higher education. The more understanding institutional leaders have about the what, when, and how of organizational change, the better equipped they will be to confront challenges and possible resistance to an evolving HSI identity.

## Notes

1. The terms Hispanic and Latino are used interchangeably throughout the chapter.
2. Santiago and Galdeano (2015) define posttraditional students as those who may need academic prep, enroll at 2-year colleges, are part time, delay enrollment, live off campus, take more than 4 years to complete college, work 30 hours or more, and make college choices based on cost, location, and accessibility.

## References

Contreas, F. E., Malcom, L. E., & Bensimon, E. M. (2008). Hispanic-serving institutions: Closeted identity and the production of equitable outcomes for Latino/a students. In M. Gasman, B. Baez, & C. Sotello Virenes Turner (Eds.), *Understanding minority-serving institutions* (pp. 71–90). Albany: State University of New York Press.

Damore, D. (2014). Held harmless: Higher education funding and the 77th session of the Nevada legislature. *The Lincy Institute Policy Brief*. Retrieved from http://www.unlv.edu/sites/default/files/page_files/31/Lincy-HeldHarmless.pdf

Gasman, M. (2008). Minority-serving institutions: A historical backdrop. In M. Gasman, B. Baez, & C. Sotello Virenes Turner (Eds.), *Understanding minority-serving institutions* (pp. 18–27). Albany: State University of New York Press.

Hebel, S. (2010, March 14). State cuts are pushing public colleges into peril. *Chronicle of Higher Education*. Retrieved from http://chronicle.com/article/In-Many-States-Public-High/64620/

Higher ed reality: Large tuition subsidies aren't coming back. [Editorial]. (2011, January 19). *Las Vegas Review Journal*. Retrieved from http://www.reviewjournal.com/opinion/editorials/higher-ed-reality-large-tuition-subsidies-arent-coming-back

Kezar, A. J. (2001). *Understanding and facilitating organizational change in the 21st century: Recent research and conceptualizations* [ASHE-ERIC Higher Education Report, 28(4)]. San Francisco, CA: Jossey-Bass.

Kezar, A., Carducci, R., & Contreras-McGavin, M. (2006). *Rethinking the "L" word in higher education: The revolution of research on leadership* [ASHE Higher Education Report, 31(6)]. San Francisco, CA: Jossey-Bass.

León, D. J. (Ed.). (2003). *Latinos in higher education*. London, UK: Elsevier.

Martinez, M. (2011). *2010 diversity in Nevada public higher education*. Reno: Nevada System of Higher Education. Retrieved from http://system.nevada.edu/tasks/sites/Nshe/assets/File/Academics/reports/diversity/Report_on_NSHE_Diversity_2010.pdf

Martinez, M. (2014). Understanding Nevada's higher education governance for two-year colleges: Challenges and solutions. *The Lincy Institute Policy Brief*. Retrieved from https://www.unlv.edu/sites/default/files/24/LincyInstitute-UnderstandingNevadasHigherEducationGovernanceForTwoYearColleges.pdf

Martinez, M., Damore, D. F., & Lang, R. E. (2014). The case for a new college governance structure in Nevada: Integrating higher education with economic development. *The Lincy Institute Policy Brief*. Retrieved from http://www.unlv.edu/sites/default/files/50/LincyInstitute-TheCaseForANewCollegeGovernanceStructureInNevada.pdf

McLendon, M. K., & Hearn, J. C. (2007). Incorporating political indicators into comparative-state study of higher education policy: Opportunities and limitations of space and time. In K. Shaw & D. E. Heller (Eds.), *The challenges of comparative state-level higher education policy research* (pp. 11–36). Sterling, VA: Stylus.

Myers, D. (2011, February 3). Educators: Heath Morrison and Dan Klaich. *Reno News & Review, Opinions*. Retrieved from https://www.newsreview.com/reno/educators/content?oid=1916489

Nevada Department of Education. (n.d.). *Annual reports college-going and college credit accumulation*. Retrieved from http://www.doe.nv.gov/DataCenter/Annual_Rpts_College_Going_College_Credit_Accum_Rates/

Nevada Legislative Counsel Bureau. (2013a). *2013 Nevada education data book*. Research Division of the Legislative Counsel Bureau. Retrieved from http://www.leg.state.nv.us/Division/Research/Publications/EdDataBook/2013/2013EDB.pdf

Nevada Legislative Counsel Bureau. (2013b). *Funding of higher education* (Bulletin No. 13-08). Retrieved from https://www.leg.state.nv.us/Division/Research/Publications/InterimReports/2013/Bulletin13-08.pdf

Nevada System of Higher Education. (2012, September 7). *Cultural Diversity Committee meeting minutes*. Retrieved from http://system.nevada.edu/tasks/sites/Nshe/assets/File/BoardOfRegents/Agendas/2012/nov-mtgs/cd/CD-2.pdf

Nevada System of Higher Education. (2013, June 7). *NSHE diversity report 2011–12*. Retrieved from http://system.nevada.edu/tasks/sites/Nshe/assets/File/BoardOfRegents/Agendas/2013/jun-mtgs/cd/CD-4a.pdf

Nevada System of Higher Education. (2015). *Nevada emerging Hispanic-serving institutions*. Retrieved from http://system.nevada.edu/Nshe/index.cfm/initiatives/diversity-and-inclusion/emerging-hispanic-serving-institutions1/

Nuñez, A., Hurtado, S., & Galdeano, E. C. (Eds.). (2015). *Hispanic-serving institutions: Advancing research and transformative practice*. New York, NY: Routledge.

Pew Research Center. (2011). *Demographic profile of Hispanics in Nevada, 2011*. Retrieved from http://www.pewhispanic.org/states/state/nv/

Richardson, R. C., & de los Santos, G. E. (2001). Statewide governance structures and two-year colleges. In B. K. Townsend & S. B. Twombly (Eds.), *Community colleges: Policy in the future context* (pp. 39–56). Westport, CT: Ablex Publishing.

Santiago, D. A. (2009, September 17). Enrolling vs. serving Latino students. *Diverse Issues in Higher Education*. Retrieved from http://diverseeducation.com/article/13051/

Santiago, D. A., & Andrade, S. J. (2010). *Emerging Hispanic-serving institutions (HSIs): Serving Latino students*. Washington, DC: Excelencia in Education. Retrieved from http://files.eric.ed.gov/fulltext/ED508202.pdf

Santiago, D. A., & Galdeano, E. C. (2015). *Helping or hindering: State policies and Latino college completion*. Washington, DC: Excelencia in Education. Retrieved from http://www.edexcelencia.org/research/helping-or-hindering

Santiago, D. A., Galdeano, M. C., & Taylor, M. (2015). *Factbook 2015: The condition of Latinos in education*. Washington, DC: Excelencia in Education. Retrieved from http://www.edexcelencia.org/research/2015-factbook

Vuong, B., & Hairston, C. C. (2012). *Using data to improve minority-serving institution success*. Washington, DC: Institute for Higher Education Policy. Retrieved from http://www.ihep.org/sites/default/files/uploads/docs/pubs/mini_brief_using_data_to_improve_msi_success_final_october_2012_2.pdf

*MAGDALENA MARTINEZ is the director of education programs at the Lincy Institute and a faculty member at the University of Nevada, Las Vegas.*

# 3

*This chapter highlights the factors that hinder or contribute to the success of Latino and Latina students at predominantly White institutions. The Culturally Engaging Campus Environments (CECE) Model is offered as a framework from which to create environments for Latino/a students to thrive in college.*

# Cultivating Campus Environments to Maximize Success Among Latino and Latina College Students

*Judy Marquez Kiyama, Samuel D. Museus, Blanca E. Vega*

According to the U.S. Census Bureau (2012), because of the continued steady growth of Latino/a communities in the United States, this population now represents the country's largest racial or ethnic minority group at 17% or 53 million people. At the same time, Latino/a students continue to face racial inequities in higher education. Recent data demonstrate that Latino/a students are substantially less likely than their White peers to matriculate into a 4-year institution, attend a selective college or university, enroll in college full time, and complete a bachelor's degree (Pew Hispanic Center, 2013). Thus, it is important to understand the institutional factors that contribute to the experiences of Latino/a students, especially those enrolled at predominantly White institutions (PWIs). The purpose of this chapter is to highlight the factors that hinder or contribute to the success of Latino/a students at PWIs and to discuss how campus leaders can transform their institutional environments to maximize success among these students.

## Campus Racial Climate and Campus Racial Culture at Predominantly White Institutions

Many factors shape the experiences of Latino/a college students at PWIs, including their levels of academic preparation, pressure to fulfill family obligations, challenges navigating higher education as first-generation college students, financial challenges, gender-role stereotyping of Latinas, stress due to new and culturally exclusive curriculum, and incongruence between

New Directions for Higher Education, no. 172, Winter 2015 © 2015 Wiley Periodicals, Inc.
Published online in Wiley Online Library (wileyonlinelibrary.com) • DOI: 10.1002/he.20150

their cultural heritages and the culture of their campuses (Gloria, Castellanos, & Orozco, 2005; Lopez, 2005). In addition, there is a growing body of evidence that campus racial climates and campus racial cultures shape the experiences of Latino/a students in higher education. Whereas *campus racial climate* has been defined as "the overall racial environment" of postsecondary institutions (Solórzano, Ceja, & Yosso, 2000, p. 62), the *campus racial culture* has been defined as the following:

> the collective patterns of tacit values, beliefs, assumptions, and norms that evolve from an institution's history and are manifest in its mission, traditions, language, interactions, artifacts, physical structures, and other symbols, which differentially shape the experiences of various racial and ethnic groups and can function to oppress racial minority populations within a particular institution. (Museus, Ravello, & Vega, 2012, p. 32)

The campus racial climate and campus racial culture are both significant aspects of the campus environment, and each of them is important in efforts to develop holistic understandings of the experiences of Latino/a students at PWIs.

Several studies suggest that campus racial climates exhibit a salient influence on the experiences of many Latino/a students at PWIs (Hurtado & Carter, 1997; Hurtado & Ponjuan, 2005; Locks, Hurtado, Bowman, & Oseguera, 2008; Museus, Nichols, & Lambert, 2008; Villalpando, 2010). When compared to White peers, Latino/a students and other students of color often report that the campus climate is less welcoming or is hostile (Lowe, Byron, Ferry, & Garcia, 2013). This discrepancy is due to the reality that institutions can and often do cultivate and perpetuate hostile campus racial climates that are permeated with prejudice and discrimination, racial stereotypes, low expectations from teachers and peers, exclusion from the curriculum, and pedagogy that marginalizes or tokenizes the voices of Latino/a college students and other undergraduates of color (Castellanos & Gloria, 2007; Lopez, 2005).

There is also some indication that negative campus racial climates result in increased feelings of marginality and isolation, decreased sense of belonging, higher levels of racism-related stress, increased withdrawal from classroom participation, and lower levels of persistence and degree completion among Latino/a students (Castellanos & Gloria, 2007; Lopez, 2005). Moreover, these environmental realities are often exacerbated by low representation of Hispanic college students, faculty, and staff. Because of this persistent low representation, campuses may call upon Latino/a students to lead diversity efforts and represent the perspective of all students of color on their respective campuses (Castellanos & Gloria, 2007).

Researchers have also begun to shed light on how campus racial cultures shape the experiences of Latino/a students and other students of color at PWIs. For example, the campus racial culture of PWIs often privileges

Eurocentric cultural values, perspectives, assumptions, norms, and symbols while excluding or marginalizing the cultural backgrounds and identities of Latino/a college students (González, 2003). On the other hand, research suggests that PWIs do have the capacity to cultivate campus cultures that contribute to the conditions for Latino/a students and other undergraduates of color to thrive (Museus, 2011). For example, there is some evidence that campus cultures characterized by strong networking values, a commitment to targeted support, a belief in humanizing the educational experience, and an ethos characterized by institutional responsibility for student success are more conducive to college success among undergraduates of color.

Higher education researchers have found that the interaction between Latino/a students' home and campus cultures shape their experiences and outcomes at PWIs (Cerezo & Chang, 2013; González, 2003; Museus & Quaye, 2009). For example, greater cultural congruity, or greater fit between the cultural values that students bring to college and the dominant values of their institution, contributes to enhanced sense of belonging, academic achievement, and greater likelihood of persistence (Castellanos & Gloria, 2007; Cerezo & Chang, 2013; Gloria, Castellanos, & Orozco, 2005). Unfortunately, Latino/a college students often come from cultures that are substantially different than the ones that they encounter and must navigate on their respective campuses (González, 2003). And the burden of bridging or integrating Latino/a students' home cultures and the cultures of their campuses is often placed on the shoulders of the students themselves. Indeed, institutions often leave it up to Latino/a students to assimilate into the dominant cultures of PWIs (Hurtado & Ponjuan, 2005; Lopez, 2013). The challenges that Latino/a students face at PWIs, coupled with the continued assumption that responsibility to adjust lies primarily with these students, constitute a significant problem that warrants the attention of postsecondary educators.

Whereas the dominant cultures of PWIs often fail to reflect, and therefore frequently devalue, the cultural communities from which Latino/a students originate, these undergraduates can and do cultivate and perpetuate their own subcultures that reflect and engage their cultural communities and identities. Such subcultures provide sources of support and contribute to the conditions for those students to thrive. For example, scholars have shown how subcultures that center *familismo* as a core value can contribute to resiliency and success among Latino/a students at PWIs. The cultural concept of *familismo* includes a belief in the importance of maintaining strong family ties, the expectation that family is the primary source of support, an emphasis on loyalty to family, and a commitment to the family over individual needs (Mendoza, Hart, & Whitney, 2011). The notion of *familismo* is often extended to Latino/a peers within campus student groups as Latinos/as form a campus family or group of campus brothers and sisters. As a result, this surrogate or extended family can play an integral role in Latino/a students developing a sense of belonging, healthy identity, and the foundation for academic success in higher education (Mendoza et al., 2011; Moreno & Sanchez Banuelos, 2013). In some cases, this extended campus family is found within Latino/a Greek-letter organizations, which help these students find peer support, engage in club and organization leadership roles, and cultivate motivation to persist and graduate (Moreno & Sanchez Banuelos, 2013).

One reason subcultures that are based on core values, such as *familismo*, are important is because they allow Latino/a students to maintain critical ties to their cultural heritages while simultaneously navigating the culture of their college campuses. Indeed, evidence indicates that *familismo* and the importance that Latino/a students attach to maintaining emotional ties to their communities of origin partially determine the institutions to which these students apply and attend, and often lead them to choose campuses close to home (Kiyama, 2010; Mendoza et al., 2011; Sapp, Kiyama, & Dache-Gerbino, in press). In sum, Latino/a students' abilities to maintain connections to their cultural communities and their core cultural values represent an important source of emotional support while in college (Mendoza et al., 2011). In the following section, we discuss a model that can help mobilize campus conversations in ways that center Latino/a students' cultural communities and their cultural values in conversations about student success and integrate those critical cultural factors into institutional structures, spaces, curricula, policies, programs, practices, and activities to maximize success among these populations.

## A Model for Understanding, Assessing, and Fostering Campus Environments That Reflect and Respond to Latino/a Communities

To address the aforementioned climate and culture issues, educators can engage frameworks that allow them to (re)design campus environments that meaningfully engage the cultural identities of Latino/a students. Museus (2014) proposed the Culturally Engaging Campus Environments (CECE) Model (Figure 3.1), which is derived from over 100 interviews and 20 years of existing research on diverse student populations in college. The CECE Model suggests that culturally engaging campus environments (i.e., environments that reflect and respond to their cultural communities of students) are associated with more positive student outcomes in college.

The CECE Model posits that there are nine characteristics of culturally engaging campus environments, which can be divided into two subgroups of cultural relevance and cultural responsiveness indicators. The first five indicators of *cultural relevance* focus on the ways that institutional environments are relevant to the cultural backgrounds, communities, and identities of diverse college students:

**Figure 3.1. The Culturally Engaging Campus Environments (CECE) Model**

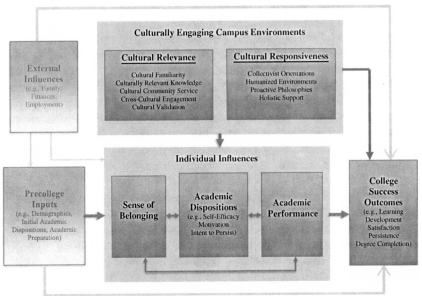

*Source:* Museus & Smith (2014).

1. **Cultural familiarity** is the extent to which college students have opportunities to physically connect with faculty, staff, and peers who understand their backgrounds and experiences.
2. **Culturally relevant knowledge** refers to opportunities for students to learn and exchange knowledge about their own cultures and communities of origin.
3. **Cultural community service** refers to the extent to which students have opportunities to engage in projects and activities to give back to and positively transform their cultural communities.
4. **Meaningful cross-cultural engagement** involves students' access to opportunities to engage in meaningful interactions with peers from diverse backgrounds to solve real social and political problems.
5. **Culturally validating environments** refer to environments that validate students' cultural knowledge, backgrounds, and identities.

The remaining four indicators of *cultural responsiveness* focus on the ways in which campus environments respond to the cultural norms and needs of diverse students:

6. **Collectivist cultural orientations** are cultural values that encourage collaboration and mutual success, rather than individualism and competition, on campus.

NEW DIRECTIONS FOR HIGHER EDUCATION • DOI: 10.1002/he

7. **Humanized educational environments** are characterized by institutional agents who care about, are committed to, and develop meaningful relationships with students.
8. **Proactive philosophies** drive the practice of institutional agents who go above and beyond making information, opportunities, and support available to encourage and sometimes pressure students to access that information, opportunities, and support.
9. **Holistic support** is characterized by the extent to which postsecondary institutions provide students with access to at least one point person—a faculty member or staff member whom those students trust to provide the information and offer the assistance that they need, or connect them with a source of support who will provide that information or assistance.

These nine indicators are based on empirical data and over 2 decades of research that link them to higher levels of engagement, sense of belonging, persistence, and degree completion (Museus, 2014). In addition, some research examining the CECE Model appears to suggest that these nine indicators are significantly correlated with key outcomes, such as sense of belonging, motivation, and self-efficacy among students of color (Museus & Smith, 2014).

Much remains to be learned about the efficacy of these indicators in promoting positive outcomes. Yet, existing evidence indicates that these nine indicators might be useful in assessing the extent to which campus environments reflect the conditions that are necessary for Latinos/as to thrive in college. Using these indicators can help educators facilitate dialogue and construct a common vision regarding the types of environments that diversity and equity initiatives should strive to achieve in order to maximize success among diverse populations. Ultimately, the CECE framework can be useful in understanding how institutions might transform or restructure their campuses and create optimal environmental conditions for these students to thrive. In the context of Latino/a student success at PWIs, the CECE Model suggests that engaging in discussions and efforts to more meaningfully cultivate campus environments that reflect and respond to Latino/a communities at PWIs might help maximize the likelihood that these students will want to engage, have positive experiences, feel a greater passion for learning, and succeed in college.

## Recommendations for Cultivating Culturally Engaging Campus Environments for Latino/a Students

In this final section, we elaborate on how PWIs can cultivate more culturally engaging campus environments by integrating the CECE indicators into their programs and practices. Although offering any holistic discussion of such transformation efforts is beyond the scope of this chapter, we provide

NEW DIRECTIONS FOR HIGHER EDUCATION • DOI: 10.1002/he

a handful of recommendations that can aid institutional leaders in advancing such agendas on their respective campuses. Due to space limitations, we focus on providing recommendations based on the indicators of cultural relevance. Many of our recommendations reinforce the sentiments of previous scholars (see Castellanos & Gloria, 2007; Ortiz, 2004) but emphasize the need to focus on holistic efforts that promote institutional transformation. For a more comprehensive discussion of the ways in which postsecondary campuses can use the CECE Model as a framework to cultivate more culturally relevant and responsive environments, we refer readers to Museus and Smith (2014).

**Creating Spaces to Find Cultural Familiarity on Campus.** College faculty, administrators, and staff should invest substantial energy in racial- and ethnic-specific campus programming that can provide undergraduates with opportunities to connect with people from similar backgrounds. One critical way in which institutions offer such support is by providing Latino/a student groups office space where they can find cultural familiarity and connect with support from peers and mentors (Harris & Kiyama, 2013). Institutions can use such physical spaces to construct culturally relevant spaces that are based on the notion of *familismo* and reflect cultural values of loyalty, solidarity, and reciprocity (Castellanos & Gloria, 2007). In addition, institutions should constantly seek new ways to engage broader Latino/a communities in their environments. For example, Metropolitan State University of Denver recently implemented *Orientación Familiar*, an orientation program designed specifically for Spanish-speaking families. The program focused on building upon family knowledge and resources while sharing examples of how to continue supporting students once they make the transition into college.

**Using Multifaceted Approaches to Engaging and Exchanging Culturally Relevant Knowledge.** The role of space is also a critical consideration within the context of academic programs. First and foremost, it is important for campuses to consider the value of Latino/a studies programs and courses as spaces where culturally relevant knowledge for the Latino/a community can be acquired and exchanged. Faculty and staff should consider compiling resources that can help Latino/a students find spaces where they can learn and exchange knowledge about their own cultural communities. For example, on campuses that do not house a Latino/a studies program, faculty and staff can construct a list of courses relevant to Latino/a studies so that students know where to access such courses upon their arrival. In addition, faculty and staff can make concerted efforts to provide Latino/a student organizations with information about other Latinos/as and more general diversity-focused scholarly events on their respective campuses.

**Providing Opportunities to Give Back to Cultural Communities.** Many Latino/a students arrive on campuses with a strong desire to provide service to their communities. To capitalize on this passion, institutions should provide a wide range of culturally relevant service-learning opportunities that are built into academic courses or cocurricular projects. Work-study opportunities could offer unique experiences embedded in Latino/a community needs, and educators should make efforts to ensure that opportunities to engage in undergraduate research projects are culturally relevant.

**Understanding and Engaging Cultural Symbols to Provide Cultural Validation.**    Making efforts to cultivate culturally validating environments can prompt institutions to review cultural symbols across campus. For example, if campuses host "fiesta nights," they could refrain from tokenizing Latino/a culture by engaging in interdisciplinary programming efforts with history or anthropology departments and student organizations. Programming efforts can offer information on the historical significance of Latino/a symbols like sombreros in Mexican mariachi song and dance or the relevance of sombreros in both Mexico and the Philippines. When institutions engage cultural aspects of Latino/a communities, it is important that they review these items with faculty, staff, and students knowledgeable of *Latinidad,* or "the diverse array of competing paradigms of identity and heterogeneous experiences of various Latino national groups" to offer a more accurate representation of Latino/a culture and therefore a more culturally validating environment (Aparicio, 1999, p. 10).

**Conducting Continuous Assessment to Inform Institutional Improvement Efforts.**    It is critical that institutional leaders engage in continuous assessment of their campus environments. For example, colleges and universities can use the CECE Survey (Museus & Smith, 2014) to better understand the extent to which they are providing the types of campus environments that allow diverse populations to thrive. The CECE Survey is a questionnaire that is derived from the CECE Model, has been tested and validated, and can be used to measure the nine CECE indicators. The data generated by the survey can continuously inform strategic planning, program evaluation and development, policy revision, and curricular reform efforts at postsecondary institutions.

## Conclusion

Although Latino/a students are members of the largest community of color in the United States, they continue to achieve college degrees at lower rates than other racial and ethnic groups. Thus, researchers and practitioners must better understand how to transform institutional environments to better serve this population. The CECE Model (Museus, 2014) provides an important tool that can prompt institutional leaders and educators to reflect on issues associated with Latino/a educational achievement and success rather than relying on students themselves for the answers. By integrating an understanding of the CECE Model and Latino/a culture into institutional environments, practitioners and researchers can be better equipped to construct policies and programs that maximize Latino/a student success in higher education.

## References

Aparicio, F. (1999). Reading the "Latino" in Latino studies: Towards reimagining our academic location. *Discourse, 21*(3), 3–18.

Castellanos, J., & Gloria, A. M. (2007). Research considerations and theoretical application for best practices in higher education: Latina and Latinos achieving success. *Journal of Hispanic Higher Education, 6*(4), 378–396.

Cerezo, A., & Chang, T. (2013). Latina and Latino achievement at predominantly White universities: The importance of culture and ethnic community. *Journal of Hispanic Higher Education, 12*(1), 72–85.

Gloria, A. M., Castellanos, J., & Orozco, V. (2005). Perceived educational barriers, cultural congruity, coping responses, and psychological well-being of Latina undergraduates. *Hispanic Journal of Behavioral Sciences, 27,* 161–183.

González, K. P. (2003). Campus culture and the experiences of Chicano students in a predominantly White university. *Urban Education, 37*(2), 193–218.

Harris, D. M., & Kiyama, J. M. (2013). The role of community and school-based programs in aiding Latina and Latino student high school persistence. *Education and Urban Society.* doi:10.1177/0013124513495274

Hurtado, S., & Carter, D. F. (1997). Effects of college transition and perceptions of campus racial climate on Latino college students' sense of belonging. *Sociology of Education, 70,* 324–345.

Hurtado, S., & Ponjuan, L. (2005). Latino educational outcomes and the campus climate. *Journal of Hispanic Higher Education, 4*(3), 235–251.

Kiyama, J. M. (2010). College aspirations and limitations: The role of educational ideologies and funds of knowledge in Mexican American families. *American Educational Research Journal, 47*(2), 330–356.

Locks, A. M., Hurtado, S., Bowman, N. A., & Oseguera, L. (2008). Extending notions of campus climate and diversity to students' transition to college. *Review of Higher Education, 31*(3), 257–285.

Lopez, J. D. (2005). Race-related stress and sociocultural orientation among Latino students during their transition into a predominantly white, highly selective institution. *Journal of Hispanic Higher Education, 4*(4), 354–365.

Lopez, J. D. (2013). Differences among Latino students in precollege multicultural exposure and transition into an elite institution. *Journal of Hispanic Higher Education, 12*(3), 269–279.

Lowe, M. R., Byron, R. A., Ferry, G., & Garcia, M. (2013). Food for thought: Frequent interracial dining experiences as a predictor of students' racial climate perceptions. *Journal of Higher Education, 84*(4), 569–600.

Mendoza, M., Hart, J., & Whitney, S. (2011). Taking the family to college: Understanding the role of family in the resiliency of Hispanic students at a predominantly White Midwest university. *Enrollment Management Journal, 5*(4), 67–90.

Moreno, D. R., & Sanchez Banuelos, S. M. (2013). The influence of Latina and Latino Greek sorority and fraternity involvement on Latina and Latino college student transition and success. *Journal of Latin/Latin American Studies, 5*(2), 113–125.

Museus, S. D. (2011). Generating Ethnic Minority Success (GEMS): A collective-cross case analysis of high-performing colleges. *Journal of Diversity in Higher Education, 4*(3), 147–162.

Museus, S. D. (2014). The Culturally Engaging Campus Environments (CECE) Model: A new theory of college success among racially diverse student populations. In

M. B. Paulsen (Ed.), *Higher education: Handbook of theory and research* (pp. 189–227). New York, NY: Springer.

Museus, S. D., Nichols, A. H., & Lambert, A. D. (2008). Racial differences in the effects of campus racial climate on degree completion: A structural equation model. *Review of Higher Education, 32*(1), 107–134.

Museus, S. D., & Quaye, S. J. (2009). Toward an intercultural perspective of racial and ethnic minority college student persistence. *Review of Higher Education, 33*(1), 67–94.

Museus, S. D., Ravello, J. N., & Vega, B. E. (2012). The campus racial culture: A critical race counterstory. In S. D. Museus & U. M. Jayakumar (Eds.), *Creating campus cultures: Fostering success among racially diverse student populations* (pp. 28–45). New York, NY: Routledge.

Museus, S. D., & Smith, E. (2014). *The Culturally Engaging Campus Environments (CECE) model and survey: New tools for assessing the impact of campus environments on diverse college student outcomes.* Washington, DC: NASPA–Student Affairs Administrators in Higher Education.

Ortiz, A. M. (2004). Promoting the success of Latino students: A call to action. In A. M. Ortiz (Ed.), *New Directions for Student Services: No. 105. Addressing the unique needs of Latino American students* (pp. 89–97). San Francisco, CA: Jossey-Bass.

Pew Hispanic Center. (2013). *Hispanic high school graduates pass Whites in rate of college enrollment.* Washington, DC: Pew Hispanic Center.

Sapp, V. T., Kiyama, J. M., & Dache-Gerbino, A. (in press). Against all odds: Latinas activate agency to secure access to college. *NASPA Journal about Women in Higher Education.*

Solórzano, D. G., Ceja, M., & Yosso, T. (2000). Critical race theory, racial microaggressions, and campus racial climate: The experiences of African-American college students. *Journal of Negro Education, 69*(1), 60–73.

U.S. Census Bureau. (2012). *2012 population estimates.* Retrieved from http://factfinder.census.gov/faces/nav/jsf/pages/index.xhtml

Villalpando, O. (2010). Latina/os in higher education: Eligibility, enrollment, and educational attainment. In E. G. Murillo, Jr., S. A. Villenas, R. T. Galvan, J. S. Munoz, C. Martinez, & M. Machado-Casas (Eds.), *Handbook of Latinos and education: Theory, research, and practice* (pp. 232–249). New York, NY: Routledge.

JUDY MARQUEZ KIYAMA *is associate professor of higher education in the Morgridge College of Education at the University of Denver.*

SAMUEL D. MUSEUS *is an associate professor of higher education and student affairs and the director of the Culturally Engaging Campus Environments (CECE) project at Indiana University, Bloomington.*

BLANCA E. VEGA *is a doctoral student in the Higher and Postsecondary Education program at Teachers College, Columbia University.*

4

*This chapter investigates the institutionalization of support for undocumented students across states that either extend or deny in-state resident tuition (ISRT) benefits. In their review, the authors highlight promising practices.*

# Institutionalizing Support for Undocumented Latino/a Students in American Higher Education

*Ryan Evely Gildersleeve, Darsella Vigil*

When seeking to support undocumented students, it is imperative to examine the implementation of policy and, in some cases, the mitigation of policies that might disenfranchise undocumented students. Further, it is important to consider the establishment of administrative infrastructures to support undocumented students' success in college. To these ends, this chapter investigates the institutionalization of support for undocumented students across two different state contexts: (a) states that extend in-state resident tuition (ISRT) benefits and (b) states that deny ISRT benefits. In examining support structures across these contexts, we make recommendations for working across social, political, and institutional contexts in support of undocumented student success in postsecondary education. We also identify promising practices that institutions might consider (e.g., DREAM Centers) and highlight potential constraints of various organizational structures (e.g., decisions about where support services are housed in the organization).

Although scholars have sought to examine the impact of ISRT policies (Flores, 2010a, 2010b; Gildersleeve & Hernández, 2012) and the experiences of undocumented students broadly (Buenavista & Gonzales, 2010; Perez Huber & Malagon, 2006), it has become apparent that additional work must be done to examine how institutions support undocumented students in higher education and how the institutionalization of support must attend to different state policy contexts. We highlight promising practices from four institutions that are in the national spotlight as innovators on the front lines of serving undocumented students. Two are in states that

New Directions for Higher Education, no. 172, Winter 2015 © 2015 Wiley Periodicals, Inc.
Published online in Wiley Online Library (wileyonlinelibrary.com) • DOI: 10.1002/he.20151

extend ISRT benefits, and two are in states that deny ISRT benefits to undocumented students. We conclude with an invitation to practitioners to engage in a conversation about the benefits and constraints of these institutional responses. We begin this conversation with our own reflections from this review of promising practices.

## Legal Context

Federal legislation has changed the political context for undocumented children and young adults nationwide. In 1982, the ruling in *Plyler v. Doe* is perhaps the most significant groundbreaking case that granted undocumented students the right to kindergarten to 12th grade (K–12) education (Gonzales, 2009; Olivas, 2012). Although this ruling was a victory for undocumented families in the United States, public benefits did not extend to postsecondary education (Rincon, 2008). This positioned undocumented students as international students, making it significantly more difficult for them to access and finance their college education.

In an effort to make higher education more accessible and affordable, some states have adopted laws that extend in-state resident tuition to undocumented students. ISRT policies afford undocumented students the right to pay tuition at the same rate as a local resident at any public postsecondary institution (Gildersleeve, Rumann, & Mondragón, 2012). However, it is important to recognize that the legislative bill does not grant undocumented students the right to receive any federal financial aid. To date, there are 20 states that grant undocumented students IRST benefits and 9 states that restrict these benefits.

Since 2001, the DREAM Act remains the only federal legislative bill that provides undocumented students a pathway to citizenship through the participation of college or the armed services. The Deferred Action for Childhood Arrivals (DACA) program, passed in 2012, grants qualifying undocumented students, ages 15 to 30, temporary immigration status, which temporarily relieves them from deportation while granting them a temporary work permit (United States Citizenship and Immigration Services, 2014). The DACA program does not provide a pathway to citizenship and the DREAM Act has not been passed.

## Challenges and Struggles of Undocumented Students

The most common barrier for undocumented students noted in the literature is that they do not qualify for federal or state financial aid and, depending on the state in which they reside, are required to pay nonresident tuition rates (Contreras, 2009; Flores, 2010a; Frum, 2007; Gonzales, 2009). Nonresident tuition rates are typically two to seven times higher than tuition rates for in-state residents (Feder, 2008; Olivas, 2012). The impact of these exceptionally high rates of tuition combined with little to no financial assistance is exacerbated when considering undocumented students' socioeconomic status.

Undocumented college students often lack the means to afford the cost of college (Contreras, 2009; Green, 2003). Most are from low-income backgrounds and are first in their family to attend college (Abrego, 2006; Flores, 2010b; Oliverez, 2006). Frum (2007) states, "39% of undocumented children live below the federal poverty level (compared to 17% of native-born children) while the average income of an undocumented immigrant's family is 40% lower than that of either native-born families or legal immigrant families" (p. 81). Additionally, the option to finance their education with scholarships diminishes dramatically when undocumented students learn that many scholarships require proof of legal residency in order to be eligible (Contreras, 2009; Oliverez, 2006). With limited or no access to federal loans, grants, work-study, and scholarships, undocumented students are left to pay for college with their own economic means. These findings are consistent throughout the literature, often highlighting the fact that undocumented students generally cannot work legally in the United States to offset their college costs (Abrego, 2006; Contreras, 2009; Pérez, 2010; Perez Huber & Malagon, 2006; Rincon, 2008).

## Role of Faculty and Administrators

Administration and faculty play critical roles in how undocumented students experience college. The most common institutional constraint in the research literature is how frequently undocumented students receive incorrect information from faculty and administration across all levels of education, including K–12 schools and higher education institutions (Contreras, 2009; Gonzales, 2008; Oliverez, 2006; Perez & Rodriguez, 2011). Perez and Rodriguez (2011) found that undocumented students' psychological stress was made worse by university agents who were unfamiliar with policies regarding undocumented students' rights. Undocumented students express difficulty interacting with and trusting faculty members and administrators when they need help (Contreras, 2009; Pérez, Cortés, Ramos, & Coronado, 2010; Pérez, Espinoza, Ramos, Coronado, & Cortés, 2009). Yet, college administrators and faculty members can provide some of the most successful support. Studies have shown that supportive and sensitive staff who are knowledgeable about state policies and institutional practices can counter the negative and discriminatory messages undocumented students receive (Chen, Budianto, & Wong, 2010; Contreras, 2009; Perez & Rodriguez, 2011; Pérez et al., 2010). However, researchers warn that colleges and universities are doing little to institutionalize support and services to meet the unique needs of their undocumented students.

## Promising Practices That Institutionalize Support for Undocumented Student Success

We describe efforts from two flagship institutions in states with longstanding ISRT policies that extend in-state tuition and some financial aid to undocumented students: Texas and California. These cases were chosen because of their extensive online presence and the first author's firsthand familiarity with each. We then turn our attention to two cases from states with policies that restrict higher education benefits from undocumented students: Arizona and Georgia. These cases were chosen to demonstrate how student support services can be organized in anti-immigrant contexts. None of these four cases is presented as a result of a disciplined and rigorous inquiry. Rather, we offer our synthesis of these programs based on publicly available information, highlighting the promising practices of each in relation to the constraints and recommendations reviewed earlier from previous research literature and in their specific state and institutional contexts.

**Extending State Contexts.**    This section includes examples from the University of Texas at Austin and UCLA.

*The International Office at the University of Texas at Austin.*    Texas is home to approximately 1.7 million undocumented immigrants, second only to California (Passel, Cohn, & Gonzalez-Barrera, 2013). Texas was the first state to legislate ISRT benefits for undocumented students via House Bill 1403 in 2001, just 5 years following the passage of the federal 1996 Illegal Immigration Reform and Immigrant Responsibility Act. There was much contention after HB 1403 went into effect. Some deemed it unconstitutional as it allowed certain individuals to be treated differently than others. Thus, in 2005, Senate Bill 1528 was passed amending the provisions in HB 1403 and affording residency benefits to all individuals who had resided in Texas for at least 3 years leading up to a high school diploma or general equivalency diploma (GED). This included citizens, permanent residents, and some international students (Texas Higher Education Coordinating Board, 2008). As of the time of printing, Texas is one of only five states that offer financial aid to its undocumented students. In 2011, over 16,000 students attended college under HB 1403—75% at community colleges and 25% at 4-year institutions (Texas Comptroller of Public Accounts, 2006; University of Texas at Austin, 2014).

The University of Texas at Austin (UT) is the largest campus in the University of Texas System. Institutional services dedicated to supporting undocumented students are consolidated as the "Longhorn Dreamers Project," which is a collaborative effort between UT's International Student and Scholar Services (ISSS) and University Leadership Initiative (University of Texas at Austin, 2014). The Longhorn Dreamers Project is housed in the International Student and Scholar Services division of the International Office at UT. It provides comprehensive support to undocumented students, including administrative, academic, and wellness services. It offers

New Directions for Higher Education • DOI: 10.1002/he

resources for students before and during college and after graduation. Most of these resources are informational and provide accurate and timely information for undocumented students about studying at UT. Information focuses on the application process for precollege students, financial aid, student life, health for current students, graduate school admissions, and employment for graduates. The project also refers students to health, legal, and academic services. Some direct services, such as a mandatory orientation for all HB 1403 students, are also provided through the project.

From an institutional perspective, perhaps the most valuable resources the Longhorn Dreamers Project provides are advisors and counselors at UT. College administrators are often unaware or uninformed about their responsibilities to undocumented students as well as what accurate information is needed to support them effectively (Dougherty, Nienhusser, & Vega, 2010; Nienhusser, 2014). The Longhorn Dreamers Project makes it perfectly clear that undocumented students have the right to attend UT and, therefore, should receive advising and other services to support their success. The Longhorn Dreamers Project prompts advisors to become informed and disseminates resources with accurate information about admissions, employment, financial resources, and relevant laws and policies, such as DACA. Further, the Longhorn Dreamers Project connects interested campus individuals with other campus, regional, and national activist efforts.

Although the Longhorn Dreamers Project at UT exists largely as a virtual space with online information, referrals, and only minimal direct services to students, faculty, or administrators, it provides essential support for undocumented students. Additionally, a number of workshops, guest speakers, and special-issues events are sponsored or cosponsored through the ISSS, creating a space to institutionalize sustainable support for undocumented students.

*IDEAS and the Undocumented Student Program at UCLA.*    According to Nwosu and Batalova (2015), undocumented students in California represent 25% of all undocumented students residing in the United States and 6.8% of the total California population. In 2001, the California legislature was the second to pass an in-state resident tuition law, Assembly Bill 540 (AB 540) (Abrego, 2008). In 2011, the state legislature passed the California Dream Act, which included provisions for some state aid to be made available to undocumented students. The University of California–Los Angeles (UCLA) enrolls approximately 42,000 students—about 70% of whom are students of color, with Asian American (approximately 34%) and Hispanic (approximately 18%) being the largest non-White racial/ethnic populations (UCLA, 2014).

UCLA is home to a student group, Improving Dreams Equality Access and Success (IDEAS), which has been at the forefront of immigrant rights activism on college campuses across California for over a decade. IDEAS provides unofficial resources to students within their grassroots organizational capacity, including peer-to-peer support, information, and workshops about current law, policy, and processes related to AB 540, and student activism. As an institutional response, UCLA established the undocumented student project, an office in the Bruin Resource Center (housed within the Division of Student Affairs). The office is staffed by a full-time coordinator for undocumented student programs and can draw on expertise and support from other student affairs specialists. In addition to providing campus-based resources, the undocumented student project at UCLA keeps current and former stories from undocumented students on its website to raise awareness, build community, and recognize the activist orientation of many students. Material resources include question and answer pages for undergraduate and graduate AB 540 students as well as an exhaustive list of community resources focused on undocumented immigrant services (UCLA, n.d.).

**Restricting State Contexts.**   This section includes examples from ScholarshipsA-Z in Arizona and Freedom University in Georgia.

*ScholarshipsA-Z in Arizona.*   Arizona's anti-immigrant legislation and enforcement practices make it one of the most potentially dangerous contexts for immigrants in the United States today. Arizona public colleges and universities are no exception. With the passage of Proposition 300 in 2006, Arizona restricted in-state resident tuition benefits for undocumented students (Dougherty, Nienhusser, & Vega, 2010). Simultaneously, Arizona is where some of the most progressive and well-organized immigrant rights groups are located. Although various anti-immigrant laws make it difficult for institutions of higher education to openly and accessibly serve as advocates for undocumented students within the institution, the political dynamic of southern Arizona has sprung forth with powerful populist responses. One such response has been spearheaded by a team of students and advisors: ScholarshipsA-Z, a local nonprofit with national reach and a strong online presence (ScholarshipsA-Z, 2014). ScholarshipsA-Z focuses on making postsecondary opportunities available to all students, regardless of immigration status. Through its website, students, families, and concerned educators can access resources, such as personal advising sessions, school outreach projects, as well as training on relevant immigration law and school support strategies. ScholarshipsA-Z works with institutional actors but from outside the institution itself.

*Freedom University in Georgia.*   The state of Georgia legislatively restricts tuition benefits for undocumented students. The Georgia Board of Regents in 2010 adopted Policy 413, precluding undocumented students from attending the state's five most competitive institutions (Freedom University, 2011). In response, a group of faculty, students, and activists founded Freedom University, an alternative educational space where faculty members offer courses for free to undocumented students. Freedom University, in many ways, is a legacy of civil rights era freedom schools that sought to provide teaching and learning opportunities to Black children and youth. Mostly composed of humanities and social sciences, the courses do not carry credit, yet stand in the face of adversity on behalf of students seeking to further their education and their knowledge (Freedom University, 2011). Munoz, Espino, and Antrop-Gonzalez (2014) suggest that Freedom University provides a counterspace and sanctuary for undocumented students. In their analysis, the resources provided are not so much instrumental as symbolic. Taken to a radical logical end, Freedom University might afford epistemic support for undocumented students. Among our review of services in this chapter, Freedom University stands out as a noninstitutional response to an unsupportive campus climate and system policy.

## Powerful Praxis—Reflections on the Institutionalization of Systemic Supports for Undocumented Students

In reflection on what this chapter has highlighted, we present recommendations to strengthen institutional and systemic supports for undocumented students. First, in recognition of frontline administrators' influence on undocumented students' experiences, we recommend that colleges and universities develop and facilitate training about the rights of undocumented students in their state contexts, as well as cultural sensitivity training that recognizes the potential consequences of unforeseen prejudice. Institutions should examine their nondiscrimination policies and ensure the protection of all immigrant groups, regardless of their immigration status. Hiring procedures can include inquiry about potential staff members' sensitivity to immigrant issues and willingness to serve all students, including those who are undocumented.

Second, campus diversity offices can dedicate staff to serving undocumented students. Working directly with undocumented groups on campus can help colleges and universities identify available services. Research confirms that accurate, efficient, and caring academic and personal advising for undocumented students can help them be successful.

Third, to effect institutional and systemic change, staff can reach across campus departments to create awareness and educate other offices about undocumented students, policies, and resources. In contexts where state law or institutional policies express anti-immigrant sentiment, it can be useful to partner with community organizations, such as ScholarshipsA-Z or Freedom University.

Fourth, the significance of a proactive online presence cannot be understated. Three of our four featured examples maintain online resources, including social networking activities. Online environments afford opportunities to present comprehensive references to local and institutional support systems. Social media can play an invaluable role in sharing resources and support strategies across institutions and communities.

Finally, it is important to recognize that supportive environments are built from students' earliest experiences in college and need to be fostered on an ongoing basis. UCLA offers a special orientation for undocumented students, immediately opening up lines of communication and demonstrating the safe spaces that the undocumented student project and IDEAS seek to foster. The University of Texas tries to identify students early and reaches out at strategic points throughout their undergraduate experience. Freedom University in Georgia provides ongoing interaction and an open door to all students seeking to engage in learning.

## Conclusion

Institutional and systemic support for undocumented student success, from a research and practice perspective, is a new concern across postsecondary institutions. Although little research literature exists on how best to provide effective student support to undocumented students, we have provided a synthesis about undocumented student experiences across different policy contexts, and we have culled some promising practices that might prove useful to campus leaders and practitioners. We offer glimpses into four institutional contexts that have strategically developed support systems dedicated to undocumented students. Ultimately, institutions and their systems are created by individuals, and supporting undocumented student success in American higher education must begin with professionally minded, equity-oriented, and thoughtful actions from administrators and faculty in concert with undocumented students.

## References

Abrego, L. J. (2006). "I can't go to college because I don't have papers": Incorporation patterns of Latino undocumented youth. *Latino Studies, 4*, 212–231.

Abrego, L. J. (2008). Legitimacy, social identity, and the mobilization of law: The effects of Assembly Bill 540 on undocumented students in California. *Law & Social Inquiry, 33*(3), 709–734.

Buenavista, T. L., & Gonzales, J. B. (2010). DREAMs deterred: Filipino experiences and an anti-militarization critique of the development, relief, and education for alien minors act. *Asian American Policy Review, 21*, 29–37.

Chen, E. C., Budianto, L., & Wong, K. (2010). Professional school counselors as social justice advocates for undocumented immigrant students in group work. *The Journal for Specialists in Group Work, 35*(3), 255–261.

Contreras, F. (2009). Sin papeles y rompiendo barreras: Latino students and the challenges of persisting in college. *Harvard Educational Review, 79*(4), 610–631.

Dougherty, K. J., Nienhusser, K. H., & Vega, B. E. (2010). Undocumented immigrants and state higher education policy: The politics of in-state tuition eligibility in Texas and Arizona. *Review of Higher Education, 34*(1), 123–173.

Feder, J. (2008). *Unauthorized alien students, higher education, and in-state tuition rates: A legal analysis* (RS22500) [Electronic version]. Washington, DC: Congressional Research Service. Retrieved from http://digitalcommons.ilr.cornell.edu/key_workplace/550/

Flores, S. M. (2010a). State dream acts: The effect of in-state resident tuition policies and undocumented Latino students. *Review of Higher Education, 33*(2), 239–283.

Flores, S. M. (2010b). The first state dream act: In-state resident tuition and immigration in Texas. *Educational Evaluation and Policy Analysis, 32*(4), 435–455.

Freedom University. (2011). *Our mission* [Web page]. Retrieved from http://www.freedomuniversitygeorgia.com/mission.html

Frum, J. (2007). Postsecondary educational access for undocumented students: Opportunities and constraints. *American Academic, 3,* 81–108.

Gildersleeve, R. E., & Hernández, S. (2012). Producing (im)possible peoples: A critical discourse analysis of in-state resident tuition policy. *International Journal of Multicultural Education, 14*(2). Retrieved from http://www.ijme-journal.org/index.php/ijme/article/view/517/745

Gildersleeve, R. E., Rumann, C., & Mondragón, R. (2010). Serving undocumented students: Current law and policy. In J. Price (Ed.), *New Directions for Student Services: No. 131. Understanding and supporting undocumented students* (pp. 5–18). San Francisco, CA: Jossey-Bass.

Gonzales, R. G. (2008). Left out but not shut down: Political activism and the undocumented student movement. *Northwestern Journal of Law and Social Policy, 3*(2), 1–21.

Gonzales, R. G. (2009). *Young lives on hold: The college dreams of undocumented students.* New York, NY: College Board Advocacy. Retrieved from http://professionals.collegeboard.com/profdownload/young-lives-on-hold-college-board.pdf

Green, P. E. (2003). The undocumented: Educating the children of migrant workers in America. *Bilingual Research Journal, 27*(1), 51–71.

Munoz, S., Espino, M., & Antrop-Gonzalez, R. (2014). Creating counter-spaces of resistance and sanctuaries of learning and teaching: An analysis of Freedom University. *Teachers College Record, 116,* 070307.

Nienhusser, H. K. (2014). Role of community colleges in the implementation of postsecondary education enrollment policies for undocumented students. *Community College Review, 42*(1), 3–22.

Nwosu, C., & Batalova, J. (2015). *Frequently requested statistics on immigrants and immigration in the United States.* Migration Policy Institute. Retrieved from http://www.migrationpolicy.org/article/frequently-requested-statistics-immigrants-and-immigration-united-states#1

Olivas, M. A. (2012). *No undocumented child left behind: Plyler v Doe and the education of undocumented schoolchildren.* New York: NYU Press.

Oliverez, P. M. (2006). *Ready but restricted: An examination of the challenges of college access and financial aid for college-ready undocumented students in the US.* Unpublished doctoral dissertation, University of Southern California.

Passel, J. S., Cohn, D., & Gonzalez-Barrera, A. (2013). *Population decline of unauthorized immigrants stalls, may have reversed.* Pew Research Center. Retrieved from http://www.pewhispanic.org/2013/09/23/population-decline-of-unauthorized-immigrants-stalls-may-have-reversed/

Perez, P. A., & Rodriguez, J. L. (2011). Access and opportunity for Latina/o undocumented college students: Familial and institutional support factors. *Journal of the Association of Mexican American Educators, 5*(1), 14–21.

Pérez, W. (2010). Higher education access for undocumented students: Recommendations for counseling professionals. *Journal of College Admission, 206,* 32–35.

Pérez, W., Cortés, R. D., Ramos, K., & Coronado, H. (2010). "Cursed and blessed": Examining the socioemotional and academic experiences of undocumented Latina and Latino college students. In J. Price (Ed.), *New Directions for Student Services: No. 131. Understanding and supporting undocumented students* (pp. 35–51). San Francisco, CA: Jossey-Bass.

Pérez, W., Espinoza, R., Ramos, K., Coronado, H., & Cortés, R. (2009). Academic resilience among undocumented Latino students. *Hispanic Journal of Behavioral Sciences, 31*(2), 149–181.

Perez Huber, L., & Malagon, M. C. (2006). Silenced struggles: The experiences of Latina and Latino undocumented college students in California. *Nevada Law Journal*, 7, 841.

Rincon, A. (2008). *Undocumented immigrants and higher education: Sí se puede!*. New York, NY: LFB Scholarly Publishing.

ScholarshipsA-Z. (2014). *Programs* [Web page]. Retrieved from http://www.scholarshipsaz.org/resources/programs/

Texas Comptroller of Public Accounts. (2006). *Undocumented immigrants in Texas: A financial analysis of the impact to the state budget and economy*. Retrieved from http://www.coloradoimmigrant.org/downloads/TX%20Study%20on%20Undocumented%20Immigrants%20and%20Economy.pdf

Texas Higher Education Coordinating Board. (2008). *Residency and in-state tuition. Overview*. Retrieved from http://www.thecb.state.tx.us/reports/PDF/1528.PDF

United States Citizenship and Immigration Services. (2014). *Official website of the Department of Homeland Security* [Web page]. Retrieved from http://www.uscis.gov/

University of California–Los Angeles (UCLA). (2014). *Quick facts about UCLA* [Web page]. UCLA Undergraduate Admission. Retrieved from https://www.admissions.ucla.edu/campusprofile.htm

University of California–Los Angeles (UCLA). (n.d.). *Undocumented student program* [Web page]. UCLA Bruin Resource Center. Retrieved from http://www.ab540.ucla.edu/

University of Texas at Austin. (2014). *Who is undocumented?* [Web page]. International Student & Scholar Services. Retrieved from https://world.utexas.edu/isss/students/dreamers/who-is-undocumented

*RYAN EVELY GILDERSLEEVE is an associate professor and program coordinator of the Higher Education program in the Morgridge College of Education at the University of Denver.*

*DARSELLA VIGIL is a PhD student in the higher education program in the Morgridge College of Education at the University of Denver.*

NEW DIRECTIONS FOR HIGHER EDUCATION • DOI: 10.1002/he

5

*This chapter discusses a mixed-methods study of personal and programmatic factors that affected persistence of Latina graduate engineering students at a Hispanic-serving institution (HSI). The study's findings enabled us to share recommendations that may be useful to HSIs and other colleges and universities.*

# "*A pesar de todo*" (Despite Everything): The Persistence of Latina Graduate Engineering Students at a Hispanic-Serving Institution

*Sandra Aguirre-Covarrubias, Eduardo Arellano, Penelope Espinoza*

The problem of underrepresentation of women in engineering motivated us to explore how Latina graduate engineering students experienced a set of persistence factors at a Hispanic-serving institution (HSI). The problem of underrepresentation is important given that 25% of all U.S. scientists and engineers will be near the age of retirement by 2017 (Kettani, 2009), thus creating a potential national shortage. Women and minority groups are an important source of future engineers that can help overcome the impending shortage (Kettani, 2009). However, research shows that undergraduate female engineering students are more likely than male students to discontinue their studies after the first 2 years (Bottomley, Rajala, & Porter, 1999; Seymour & Hewitt, 1997). Research also shows that there are various reasons for the underrepresentation of female engineering students such as performance pressures; lack of role models; financial difficulties (Hartman & Hartman, 2006); issues of confidence and discrimination (Bottomley et al., 1999; Hall & Sandler, 1982); and stereotypes, stress, and feelings of isolation (Anderson-Rowland, Bernstein, & Russo, 2007). The problem of female underrepresentation in engineering exists at all degree levels and in the workforce, but recent trends indicate a growing interest and participation in engineering among women and minorities, Latinas in particular.

Together, Latinos/as earned 6.9% of bachelor's degrees, 3.7% of master's degrees, and 2.7% of doctorates in engineering in 2010 (National Action Council for Minorities in Engineering [NACME], 2012). They earned more degrees in engineering at all levels compared to other underrepresented minority groups (URM), including Black and American Indian

NEW DIRECTIONS FOR HIGHER EDUCATION, no. 172, Winter 2015 © 2015 Wiley Periodicals, Inc.
Published online in Wiley Online Library (wileyonlinelibrary.com) • DOI: 10.1002/he.20152

students (National Science Foundation [NSF], 2013). Also, Latinas accounted for a higher proportion of undergraduate degrees in engineering earned by their gender group, compared to Latinos. In 2010, Latinas accounted for 8.1% of all bachelor's degrees in engineering earned by women; in comparison Latinos earned 6.7% of all engineering bachelor's degrees earned by men (NACME, 2012). Additionally, URM females earned more than half of the science and engineering degrees awarded to their respective racial/ethnic groups in 2010 (NSF, 2013). Yet, minorities, and Latinas in particular, earn a greater share of undergraduate degrees in engineering compared to their share of graduate degrees. Although our primary concern is Latina representation in engineering, this fact also limits Latino representation (NACME, 2012). Data from 2008 indicate distinct patterns in employment for Latino/a engineers by degree level and gender: 65.4% of Latinas and 64.7% of Latinos holding bachelor's degrees in engineering were employed in a degree-related field. At the master's level, employment in their field was 23.1% for Latinas and 21.9% for Latinos. Such data point to a need for increased participation of Latinas and Latinos in engineering beyond the undergraduate degree level (NACME, 2012).

According to recent data, minority-serving institutions (MSIs) enroll a substantial proportion of minority students in science and engineering programs, but the percentage of Latinas and Latinos earning science and engineering bachelor's degrees at HSIs has declined between 2001 and 2010 (NSF, 2013). In line with national trends, from 2006 to 2011, women made up 20% of undergraduate engineering students at the particular HSI we studied, and the percentage of female master's engineering students decreased from 25% percent in Fall 2008 to 21% in Fall 2011. At the doctoral level, the percentage of female engineering students decreased from 30% in Fall 2008 to 19% in Fall 2011. Yet interestingly, according to NACME, the HSI in our current study awarded the third most engineering bachelor's degrees in the nation (153) to Latina and Latino students in 2011 (NACME, 2012). As a whole, current data suggest it is worthwhile to explore issues of persistence among Latinas in graduate engineering programs, especially given that the majority of our study participants were Latinas.

## Prior Research

A number of single-institution studies have provided reasons for the underrepresentation of female students in engineering. Other studies have suggested strategies to recruit and retain female students (Bottomley, Rajala, & Porter, 1999; Cordova-Wentling & Camacho, 2006; Litzler & Lange, 2006; Meadows, Nidiffer, Ball, Davis, Finelli, & Schultz, 2006). These studies shaped ours, but none more so than the study performed by Cordova-Wentling and Camacho in 2006. Cordova-Wentling and Camacho addressed the challenges for females in pursuing undergraduate engineering degrees by focusing on university, personal, and family factors that hindered

NEW DIRECTIONS FOR HIGHER EDUCATION • DOI: 10.1002/he

or assisted female students. And, like the Bottomley et al. and the Meadows et al. studies, Cordova-Wentling and Camacho used a mixed-methods approach—a survey and focus groups. However, unlike the Bottomley et al. and the Meadows et al. studies, which studied female students at the beginning and middle of their programs, Cordova-Wentling and Camacho's study focused on female engineering students who were graduating.

Cordova-Wentling and Camacho's (2006) survey found that the primary university factors that hindered female students were ineffective professors who did not motivate students. The personal factors that hindered students were lack of free time, doubts about career goals, and low self-esteem. As far as family factors were concerned, 62% of participants did not identify factors that hindered their academic decision process, and 85% did not identify factors that hindered completing their degrees. University factors that assisted students were involvement in campus student organizations and excellent professors. Personal factors that assisted students were making sure assignments were turned in on time, working hard, and studying with classmates and friends. Family factors that assisted students were support, encouragement, and financial help.

Focus group participants in Cordova-Wentling and Camacho's (2006) research reported that faculty were not supportive and approachable. Students also reported experiencing both a sense of alienation and intimidation in the classroom, which hinted at a chilly campus climate (Hall & Sandler, 1982). However, for some students these negative experiences were countered by participation in student organizations.

According to Hall and Sandler (1982, 1984), a chilly campus climate is characterized by isolation, subtle discrimination, and persistent micro-inequities experienced by women and other underrepresented groups in academic settings. However, there had been limited research on such a phenomenon in engineering. In 2006, Litzler and Lange conducted a single-institution study to assess the degree to which the campus climate differed for male and female engineering students at the undergraduate and graduate levels. This study relied on two online surveys, one for undergraduate and one for graduate students. However, the researchers did not indicate how far the students had progressed in their program of studies. Still, Litzler and Lange concluded that female students felt singled out because of their gender and that male students were favored over female students. In addition, female students felt overwhelmed by the pace and workload of engineering courses. At the undergraduate level, female students believed they were taken more seriously by faculty in the classroom than their male classmates but felt more isolated and more adversely affected by competition than their male classmates. Litzler and Lange attributed the female students' sense of isolation and negative effects of competition to the lack of working relationships with their male classmates.

At the graduate level, the study (Litzler & Lange, 2006) found that female students reported lower satisfaction in their relationships with faculty than their male classmates. Female students also reported that they were treated with less respect by their advisors and that advisors were less available for them than for male students. Female students felt that grades were not solely based on performance in the classroom. However, the survey did not give students the opportunity to explain how else grades were determined. Although female students reported experiencing more sexual harassment from their advisors, faculty, and classmates than their male classmates, the survey did not enable students to specify the kind of sexual harassment that was experienced. In sum, related studies have been conducted with undergraduate students at the beginning or middle of their programs and have not fully discussed how female students have experienced environmental factors that could affect persistence. Equally important, no study was found that focused on Latina graduate engineering students. It is with all of these factors in mind that we designed and implemented our study using the following research methods.

## Research Methods

We conducted our mixed-method study using an online survey and semistructured interviews. The survey was conducted first to help us determine the interview questions. We chose factors with the highest frequencies in the survey to include in our interviews. We also used the survey to identify and invite interview participants. The qualitative data were analyzed using grounded theory. To explore how students had experienced a group of persistence factors, we focused primarily on the factors identified by Cordova-Wentling and Camacho (2006), along with additional factors found in other studies. These factors include having a positive attitude, self-confidence, and time management skills. Other factors include experiences with faculty, advisors, and peers, and experiences with financial assistance, discrimination, and campus climate. We defined students who had persisted as those who had officially applied to graduate in the semester we conducted our study. We invited both female and male students to participate in our online survey to compare their responses and identify the most prominent factors experienced by female students, which in turn helped us formulate the questions for our semistructured interviews with female students. The online survey was also used to invite female students to participate in our interviews.

Although we interviewed female students across racial/ethnic groups, we focused on Latina students because they were the majority of our study's participants. In the semester we conducted our study, 86 students applied for graduation—60 males and 26 females. Of the 86 graduation applicants, 35 responded to our survey—22 males and 13 females. Of the 13 female respondents, 8 were Latinas, 4 were White, and 1 identified with another race or ethnicity. Seven of the eight Latinas who responded to our survey participated in our interviews, and three of those seven were international students. The remaining were domestic students—U.S. citizens or permanent residents. Three interviews were conducted in focus groups with six master's students, and one was a personal interview with the only doctoral applicant for graduation that semester.

## Findings

The survey asked students to rate the importance of factors believed to be related to persistence in their graduate engineering program. Only factors with a mean of 3.5 or greater on a scale from 1 (not at all) to 4 (a lot) were used for the interview questions. Based on this criterion, three persistence factors experienced by Latina graduate engineering students emerged: having a positive attitude ($M = 3.85$), self-confidence ($M = 3.64$), and time management skills ($M = 3.50$). In addition to these factors, other studies led us to interview female students about discrimination, campus climate, and experiences with faculty, advisors, peers, and financial aid.

**Latina Experiences with Positive Attitude, Self-Confidence, and Time Management.** When asked specifically to describe how having a positive attitude helped Latinas persist, the interviewees reported that having a positive attitude helped them overcome some of their challenges. And, although the challenges varied from student to student and from program to program, most of them concurred that having a positive attitude helped to overcome obstacles. However, there were also a few Latinas who, instead of answering how having a positive attitude helped them persist, explained what positive attitude meant to them, described what they associated it with, or reflected on its impact.

When asked to describe how having self-confidence helped them, most stated that it played a key role because they faced challenging programs and difficult courses or programs that were not fully established, but mostly, because they were away from their families, which they credited as their source of self-confidence. However, there were also some Latinas who, rather than describing how self-confidence helped them persist, described their struggles because of a lack of self-confidence.

When asked to describe how their time-management skills helped them persist, they reported different points of view regarding their time-management skills, with almost half of them focusing on describing how difficult it was to manage their time. Some wondered how they handled all the activities they were dealing with. Others wrestled with their time-management skills, and a few of them expressed learning to manage their time at an early age, at home, during high school, or while at college. Some of them preferred to prioritize and complete tasks in advance to avoid stress and be successful.

**Latina Experiences with Faculty, Advisors, and Peers.** Most Latinas reported having positive experiences with faculty instructors—experiences that were characterized by faculty who had open-door policies, provided academic and personal advice, were supportive and encouraging, served as mentors and coaches, but also had high expectations and were, at times, demanding. In the faculty's capacity as advisors, Latinas reported different experiences that included difficult academic relationships and lack of support to participate in summer internship opportunities. While several Latinas reported that advisors would not take their opinions or feedback into account, others experienced a lack of communication with advisors and having advisors that were unreachable. Because of the advisors' hectic schedules, some Latinas felt that their advisors were not fully supportive of their research. The Latina doctoral student who participated in our study reported not having an advisor at the beginning of her program. When she was assigned an advisor, she felt his support was not very strong. Three of the Latinas experienced a difficult academic relationship with their advisors. All of them, except for one, felt that their advisors did not listen to them. Only one Latina experienced a positive academic relationship with her advisor.

As for peer experiences, Latinas described male peers who were friendly, supportive, and competitive. In addition, Latinas reported having to "prove themselves" to gain their male peers' respect in the classroom and in the lab. Furthermore, Latinas reported feeling isolated because of the low number of female students enrolled, the lack of camaraderie, and the level of competitiveness among students.

**Latina Experiences with Financial Assistance, Discrimination, and Campus Climate.**    Several Latinas reported a lack of financial support: not receiving tuition waivers, teaching/research assistantships, scholarships, or stipends. Those who did receive financial support claimed that it was not enough to cover their academic expenses. Some Latinas struggled to make ends meet, despite working. Sometimes they worked in more than one job to finance their studies. When asked to describe their experiences with discrimination, most Latinas, with the exception of one, reported having experienced no discrimination during their graduate studies. Instead, they felt welcomed, encouraged, and supported, although two students did express having experienced what they considered a sense of intimidation from their male peers. One student also reported having experienced discrimination because of her accent and because she was a woman and a single mother.

When asked to describe the campus climate, most Latinas reported that it was "fine." However, some were unhappy with the mixing of undergraduate and graduate students in graduate-level courses and others experienced what they considered a cold climate because of a lack of interaction with peers. Some Latinas made additional comments about having to be resourceful, about their family's support or lack thereof when deciding to pursue a graduate degree in engineering, and about their concern related to studying in a foreign country.

NEW DIRECTIONS FOR HIGHER EDUCATION  •  DOI: 10.1002/he

## Summary

Our findings suggest that although Latina graduate engineering students experienced many difficulties, they persisted through to graduation. Some of the difficulties that Latinas experienced included dealing with their own insecurities, feeling intimidated, having to prove themselves to male peers, and having challenging courses and faculty. However, the notion of "looking at the future" and knowing what they "wanted to accomplish" allowed some Latinas to keep a positive attitude and persist. The lone doctoral student in our study experienced an academic program with "no orientation," "no guidance," and "no financial support," which compelled her to rely on her self-confidence to persist. The other Latina students also had to rely on their self-confidence because they felt isolated, having few female peers that they could relate to in the classroom. Interestingly, the master's students credited their families as the source of their self-confidence.

Another major difficulty was time management given the Latinas' school, work, extracurricular activities, and personal lives. School took a lot of time because of its rigor, and although work took time, it was necessary because most Latinas were living on their own. Although their families provided some financial support, the support was not enough to cover all of their expenses.

Despite the many challenges the Latinas faced, faculty as instructors made their experiences positive. The students reported that faculty had open-door policies, provided both academic and personal advice, and were supportive and encouraging. At the same time, faculty were demanding and had high expectations of students. However, the Latinas' experiences with faculty as advisors were not as positive. Latinas reported not receiving support to participate in internships, their opinions not being taken into account, and a lack of communication due to advisors' hectic schedules.

In terms of peer experiences, most of the master's students reported that their male peers were competitive, whereas the doctoral student reported that her male peers were friendly and supportive. In terms of campus climate, the experiences were mixed with a welcoming and supportive climate experienced by some Latinas, whereas others reported a lack of interaction with peers.

Another major difficulty was the lack of financial support in the form of tuition waivers, teaching or research assistantships, scholarships, or stipends to help pay for their education. Regarding discrimination, only the doctoral student reported being discriminated against because of her accent, because she was a woman, and because she was a single mother. Although some Latinas reported a sense of intimidation from their male peers, most students felt welcomed, encouraged, and supported. When asked about campus climate, Latinas were generally happy except some were displeased because undergraduates were allowed to enroll in graduate courses.

## Recommendations

In response to our findings, we propose the following recommendations for HSI graduate engineering programs that want to increase the number of Latinas receiving graduate degrees.

To address the issue of lack of confidence and isolation experienced by Latina students, engineering programs should encourage the formation of a Latina graduate engineering student organization for peer support and networking. Engineering programs should also encourage Latinas to participate in currently existing campus and community events by informing them of these opportunities.

To improve experiences with faculty, engineering programs should encourage their faculty to actively participate in the design and on-going implementation of mentoring and support programs for Latinas. The mentoring and support programs should also include professional development opportunities for faculty to improve their advising.

Engineering programs should also allow faculty to propose different allocations of time dedicated to their responsibilities in teaching, research, and service in a way that is mutually beneficial to students and institutions.

To address the difficulty of challenging courses and professors, engineering programs should encourage midterm course evaluations to identify the problems students are facing and provide the academic support needed to ensure the students' academic success for the rest of the semester. In addition, engineering programs should continuously monitor and evaluate the effectiveness of their advising.

To address the lack of financial support, engineering programs should work with other institutional offices and community and professional organizations to inform Latinas in various ways of different forms of financial assistance. Engineering programs should also host financial aid workshops and guide students through different application processes. In addition, engineering programs should incentivize faculty to include student support in their research grants. And, if possible, engineering programs should offer scholarships specifically for Latina graduate engineering students.

To address the issue of time management, engineering programs should offer a series of time-management skills workshops.

Finally, to address all of the Latinas' difficulties, engineering programs should develop and implement continuous needs assessments. These assessments can help program faculty and administrators determine the academic and support services students need to maximize their likelihood of persisting. Programs can then commit the necessary resources to effectively implement those academic and support services. Equally important, institutions of higher education, HSIs specifically, should consider expanding these recommendations from the program level to campus-wide initiatives to make an even greater impact on the persistence of Latina graduate engineering students.

NEW DIRECTIONS FOR HIGHER EDUCATION • DOI: 10.1002/he

# References

Anderson-Rowland, M. R., Bernstein, B. L., & Russo, N. F. (2007). Encouragers and discouragers for domestic and international women in doctoral programs in engineering and computer science. *Proceedings of the American Society for Engineering Education*, 1–12.

Bottomley, L., Rajala, S., & Porter, R. (1999, July). *Engineering outreach teams: K–12 outreach at North Carolina State University*. Paper presented at the Frontiers in Education Conference, San Juan, PR.

Cordova-Wentling, R., & Camacho, C. (2006, June). *Women engineers: Factors and obstacles related to the pursuit of a degree in engineering*. Paper presented at the American Society for Engineering Education, Chicago, IL.

Hall, R. M., & Sandler, B. R. (1982). *The classroom climate: A chilly one for women?* Project on the Status and Education of Women. Washington, DC: Association of American Colleges.

Hall, R. M., & Sandler, B. R. (1984). *Out of the classroom: A chilly climate for women?* Project on the Status and Education of Women. Washington, DC: Association of American Colleges.

Hartman, H., & Hartman, M. (2006). Leaving engineering: Lessons from Rowan University's College of Engineering. *Journal of Engineering Education, 95*(1), 49–61.

Kettani, H. (2009, November). *The United States' challenges in science and engineering education: The Hispanic factor*. Paper presented at the 12th IASTED International Conference on Computer and Advanced Technology in Education (CATE 2009), St. Thomas, U.S. Virgin Islands.

Litzler, E., & Lange, S. E. (2006, June). *Differences in climate for undergraduate and graduate women in engineering: The effect of context*. Paper presented at the American Society for Engineering Education, Chicago, IL.

Meadows, L. A., Nidiffer, J., Ball, S. R., Davis, C. G., Finelli, C., & Schultz, W. W. (2006, October). *Work in progress: An initial assessment of the effect of the first year experience on under-represented student retention in engineering*. Paper presented at the 36th ASEE/IEEE Frontiers in Education Conference, San Diego, CA.

National Action Council for Minorities in Engineering (NACME). (2012, August). *Latinos in engineering* (Research & Policy Brief, Vol. 2, No. 5). White Plains, NY: Author. Retrieved from http://www.nacme.org/publications/research_briefs/LatinosinEngineering.pdf

National Science Foundation (NSF). (2013). *Women, minorities, and persons with disabilities in science and engineering: 2013*. Special Report (NSF Publication No. 13-304). Arlington, VA: Author. Retrieved from http://www.nsf.gov/statistics/wmpd/

Seymour, E., & Hewitt, N. M. (1997). *Talking about leaving: Why undergraduates leave the sciences*. Boulder, CO: Westview Press.

SANDRA AGUIRRE-COVARRUBIAS *is an assistant director for research in the College of Engineering at the University of Texas at El Paso.*

EDUARDO ARELLANO *is an associate professor of higher education in the Department of Educational Leadership and Foundations at the University of Texas at El Paso.*

PENELOPE ESPINOZA *is an assistant professor in the Department of Educational Leadership and Foundations at the University of Texas at El Paso.*

*This chapter examines Latino male ethnic subgroups and their college enrollment and degree completion patterns. The chapter also offers recommendations to improve Latino male ethnic subgroups' educational achievement.*

6

# Latino Male Ethnic Subgroups: Patterns in College Enrollment and Degree Completion

*Luis Ponjuan, Leticia Palomin, Angela Calise*

Research conducted in an effort to understand Latino/a students' academic achievement gaps indicates that Latino males compared to other male ethnic groups are not enrolling and completing a college credential at similar rates (Saenz & Ponjuan, 2009). Some have criticized the limitations of examining Latino/a students as a monolithic ethnic population (Garcia & Bayer, 2005), and recent national research reports have shown different postsecondary enrollment and degree completion rates within Latino male ethnic subgroups (U.S. Census Bureau, 2013b). Given these differences, higher education researchers and practitioners must better understand this multifaceted educational issue.

Due to the inherent heterogeneity of the Latino/a population, we provide an examination of Latino male ethnic subgroup differences by country of origin (that is, Mexican, Cuban, Puerto Rican, Central American, and South American) on college-related outcomes. We used educational data from national sources (for example, the U.S. Census Bureau and National Center for Education Statistics) to understand and draw comparisons between Latino male ethnic subgroups. Unfortunately, in some instances national reports did not disaggregate the data by ethnic subgroup or country of origin. The primary aim of this chapter is to examine two Latino male ethnic subgroup differences in specific postsecondary metrics: (a) college enrollment patterns and (b) college completion rates.

NEW DIRECTIONS FOR HIGHER EDUCATION, no. 172, Winter 2015 © 2015 Wiley Periodicals, Inc.
Published online in Wiley Online Library (wileyonlinelibrary.com) • DOI: 10.1002/he.20153

**Table 6.1. Percentage of 18 to 24 Year Olds Enrolled in
Degree-Granting Institutions, by Sex and Race/Ethnicity**

| Racial Group | 2000 | 2005 | 2010 | 2012 |
|---|---|---|---|---|
| Hispanic | 18.5 | 20.7 | 27.9 | 33.5 |
| White | 36.2 | 39.4 | 40.6 | 38.3 |
| Blacks | 25.1 | 28.2 | 35.2 | 33.9 |

Source: U.S. Census Bureau (2000, 2005, 2010, 2012a).

## College Enrollment Patterns of Latino Males

Over the last decade, there has been a decline in college enrollment rates
for all male racial and ethnic groups (U.S. Census Bureau, 2013a). However, upon closer examination, male college enrollment patterns differ by
racial/ethnic groups. For instance, in 2000, Hispanic males (18.5%) when
compared to White (36.2%) and Black males (25.1%) had the lowest college
enrollment rates. By 2012, however, Latino males had the greatest gains in
college enrollment rates (15%) compared to White and Black male students
(see Table 6.1). Despite these gains, Latino male students continue to trail
their male peers.

Although college enrollment rates for all male students have declined
since 2005 (Buchmann & DiPrete, 2006; Jacob, 2002), male students of
color still have the lowest college enrollment rates, which highlights a press-
ing need to understand what factors may explain these patterns for these
students, especially Latino males.

**Factors That Influence College Enrollment Patterns of Latino
Males.**    A majority of Latino male students enroll in public, 2-year colleges
(National Center for Education Statistics, 2008). Studies have revealed that
many Latino males primarily enroll in these institutions instead of 4-year
institutions due to the lack of information about attending, actual cost of
attendance, and financial aid (Fry & Taylor, 2013; Nuñez & Kim, 2012). In
states with higher Latino population rates, Latino students are more likely
to enroll in 4-year Hispanic-serving institutions (Nuñez & Kim, 2012), and
Mexican-American students are more likely than Puerto Rican students to
initially enroll in 2-year institutions (Nuñez & Crisp, 2012). Given the different enrollment patterns, we explored three primary factors that may influence Latino male college enrollment rates in 2- or 4-year institutions:
(a) the college application process, (b) the role of Latino families, and (c)
students' understanding of the financial aid application process.

*The College Application Process.*    Scholars continue to expand our understanding of the complex process of Latino/a students' college enrollment
by exploring the first step in the college enrollment process—completing a
college application. Studies have shown that Latino/a students lack essential information about the higher education application process. Typically,
they learn about the application process from others besides their parents

and attend high schools that may not have a college-going culture (Ceja, 2006; Perez & McDonough, 2008; Roderick, Coca, & Nagaoka, 2011).

In some cases, Latino males, their families, and peers lack the social capital to gain access to higher education. For example, social capital, in the context of the college application process, suggests that some students gain critical information from family, friends, and high school educational contexts (Engberg & Wolniak, 2010; Perez & McDonough, 2008). This may suggest that Latino males—in particular those from low-income families—may not know the basics for applying to college because they do not know whom to ask for help or do not have the family or educational environment that encourages them to apply. As a result, these Latino males may become discouraged and fail to apply for college not because they lack academic ability but because they lack knowledge of the process.

*The Role of Latino Families.*    Latino families practice a cultural tradition of *familismo*, which values a strong identification and attachment to immediate and extended family (Saenz & Ponjuan, 2009; Turcios-Cotto & Milan, 2013). For some Latino/a students, this cultural tradition plays a critical role in their college enrollment patterns. This mindset of Latino parents may encourage their children to stay home during their college years and attend local community colleges. Community colleges are more attractive to students because they are less expensive, are commuter institutions located near home, and have flexible class schedules (McDonough, McClafferty, & Fann, 2002). In some cases, Latino males may not attend college due to family obligations. One study found that Latino males' academic motivation was related to "giving back" to their family instead of the influence of educational aspirations that came from their mother (Ceballo, Maurizi, Suarez, & Aretakis, 2014). Two decades ago, Latino males faced the financial tensions between funding their college education and contributing to family financial demands (Lopez, 1995). Recent studies have found that Latino/a youth still have to balance their educational aspirations with their family's financial needs (Pew Hispanic Center, 2009; Turcios-Cotto & Milan, 2013).

*Students' Understanding of the Financial Aid Application Process.*    A student's financial literacy plays a critical role in his or her academic pathways to college (Starobin, Hagedorn, Purnamasari, & Chen, 2013). In particular, Hispanic families face challenges in applying for financial aid (Horn, Chen, & Chapman, 2003; McKinney & Roberts, 2012). Therefore, we focus on students' financial aid literacy—their understanding of the college financial aid application process as a critical factor that contributes to Latino male students' college enrollment. We argue that Latino male students are less likely to enroll into college if they are unsure how they will pay for their college expenses.

For many high school students, the college application process usually begins with completing the Free Application for Federal Student Aid (FAFSA) forms. In a national high school longitudinal study (HSLS), high school males indicated their knowledge of the FAFSA as part of their

**Table 6.2.  Percentage of High School Males' Knowledge of the FAFSA Application Process**

| Racial Group | Yes | No | Don't know what FAFSA is | Haven't thought about this yet | Don't know if will/would apply |
|---|---|---|---|---|---|
| **Hispanic** | 27.1 | 4.1 | 47.0 | 15.0 | 6.8 |
| **Black** | 35.1 | 6.2 | 40.9 | 11.7 | 6.1 |
| **Asian/Pacific Islander** | 26.3 | 6.0 | 54.5 | 9.3 | 3.8 |
| **White** | 21.6 | 7.5 | 51.0 | 12.9 | 7.1 |

Source: National Center for Education Statistics (2009)

college planning process (Ingels & Dalton, 2013). Although this national report did not provide Latino ethnic subgroup differences, the results provide important insights about the levels of financial aid application knowledge of male high school students. For example, only 27% of Latino males, compared to Black males (35.1%) and White males (21.6%), had knowledge of the FAFSA application process. On average, approximately 50% of all males did not know the purpose of the FAFSA application (see Table 6.2).

The HSLS report and previous studies suggest that many of these students may lack a clear understanding of how to apply for financial aid, especially the process for completing the FAFSA. Families who are completing the FAFSA for the first time often leave out important information or put it in the wrong box, which may affect the student's chances of receiving government assistance. Even when students do apply for financial aid by filling out the FAFSA, many are still unprepared and often confused about how they will pay for college (Seidel, 2014). Therefore, regardless of the particular Latino ethnic subgroup, the lack of understanding about the financial aid application process may cause many Latino males to be overwhelmed and discouraged and may negatively affect their decision to go to college.

## College Completion Rates of Latino Males

The college completion rates of Latino males and the factors influencing degree completion differ at 2-year and 4-year colleges.

**2-Year Degree Completion Trends of Latino Males.**  Latino males compared to their female peers are less likely to complete 2-year degrees (U.S. Census Bureau, 2013c). Upon closer review, we found differences between Latino male ethnic subgroups' degree completion rates at 2-year institutions. Since 2004, no more than 29% of males in any Latino ethnic subgroup earned an associate's degree or some college credit (see Table 6.3). In 2012, Mexican (17.2%) and Central American (17.4%) male students compared to other Latino male ethnic subgroups had the lowest percentage of students completing associate's degrees (U.S. Census Bureau, 2013c). In addition, we found that some Latino male groups had inconsistent trends in

**Table 6.3.  Associate's Degree or Some College Credit Completion of Latino Males by National Origin in 2004, 2007, and 2012**

| Latino Origin | 2004 | 2007 | 2012 |
|---|---|---|---|
| Mexican | 16.7 | 15.8 | 17.2 |
| Puerto Rican | 22.0 | 26.8 | 21.0 |
| Cuban | 18.4 | 20.4 | 21.2 |
| Central American | 15.4 | 14.2 | 17.4 |
| South American | 23.4 | 24.3 | 28.4 |
| Other Hispanic | 24.9 | 25.7 | 27.3 |

Source: U.S. Census Bureau (2004, 2007, 2012b)

degree completion rates. For instance, Puerto Rican males had a 4.8% increase from 2004 to 2007, but then a decrease of 5.8% from 2007 to 2012.

**4-Year Degree Completion Trends of Latino Males.**   Since 2004, the U.S. Census Bureau (2013c) has reported a significant difference in bachelor's degree completion rates among Latino male ethnic subgroups. Completion rates have increased for most Latino male subgroups, with the exception of males with Mexican and Central American origins. In 2012, Mexican (7%) and Central American (6.9%) males above the age of 25 had the lowest bachelor's degree completion rates of any Latino male subgroups. (see Table 6.4). More important, no Latino male ethnic subgroup had a bachelor's completion rate above 20%.

**Factors That Influence Degree Completion of Latino Males.**   It is important to understand why differences exist between the associate's and bachelor's degree completion rates of Latino male ethnic subgroups. Although there are many factors that may contribute to college degree completion, we focus on three factors that may explain Latino males' 2- and 4-year college completion rates: (a) disparities in financial aid packages, (b) academic experiences, and (c) college cocurricular engagement.

*Disparities in Financial Aid Packages.*   Students experience financial stress related to paying for college-related expenses (Heckman, Lim, &

**Table 6.4.  Bachelor's Degree Completion of Latino Males by National Origin in 2004, 2007, and 2012**

| Latino Origin | 2004 | 2007 | 2012 |
|---|---|---|---|
| Mexican | 6.0 | 5.9 | 7.0 |
| Puerto Rican | 8.5 | 9.3 | 12.3 |
| Cuban | 16.2 | 18.7 | 16.1 |
| Central American | 7.0 | 9.8 | 6.9 |
| South American | 23.0 | 22.7 | 19.3 |
| Other Hispanic | 14.5 | 12.8 | 15.3 |

Source: U.S. Census Bureau (2004, 2007, 2012b)

**Table 6.5. Percentage of Male Undergraduate Students Receiving Any Type of Financial Aid**

| Male Racial/Ethnic Group | Receiving Any Aid | Receiving Any Grant | Receiving Any Loans |
|---|---|---|---|
| Hispanic | 82.3 | 70.0 | 46.4 |
| Black | 90.6 | 77.0 | 65.0 |
| Asian/Pacific Islander | 63.9 | 50.4 | 36.9 |
| White | 75.2 | 58.2 | 50.3 |

Source: National Center for Education Statistics (2008)

Montalto, 2014). Scholars highlight the fact that Latino students, compared to their White peers, depend more on financial aid programs to participate in college (Crisp, Taggart, & Nora, 2014). A National Center for Education Statistics report based on the 2007–08 National Postsecondary Student Aid Study (NPSAS:08) highlighted differences among male full-time enrolled undergraduates by racial/ethnic groups. Of students receiving any type of financial aid, Latino males represented the second highest percentage (82%) (after Black males) (see Table 6.5). By contrast, Latino males (46.4%) compared to White and Black male undergraduate students (50.3% and 65%, respectively) were least likely to receive any type of student loan (see Table 6.5). Latino/a students, compared to other ethnic groups, were also more averse to funding their college education with student loans (Cunningham & Santiago, 2008).

It is still important to highlight financial aid patterns to understand how higher education institutions can help meet the needs of Latino males. The National Center for Education Statistics (2008) report highlights the fact that many Latino males rely on financial aid to attend college. In addition, many Latino males need to supplement financial aid with additional employment, which may make it more difficult for them to focus solely on their academics and lowers the probability of earning a college degree.

*Academic Experiences.*   Crisp, Taggart, and Nora (2014) highlight several key factors that influence the academic experiences of Latino males— factors that are coupled with challenges of financing their college education. In a comprehensive review of the literature on Latino/a students, they found that males achieved lower ratings compared to females in several key academic outcomes. Unfortunately, there is scant evidence to suggest the differing effects that individual psychological, sociological, or organizational factors have on Latino male ethnic subgroups. Crisp et al. state, "Less clarity was provided to the role of ethnic subgroups in predicting academic outcomes for Latina/o students" (p. 8).

Some scholars have examined how full-time and part-time enrollment may influence Hispanic males' academic experiences. Fry (2002) found that part-time college enrollment was associated with a higher risk of low degree-completion rates, whether a student attended a 2-year or 4-year institution. As mentioned earlier, because many Latino males have to balance work and college, there is greater likelihood that they will enroll in college on a part-time basis. Crisp et al. (2014) state, "Attending college full-time was also shown to be positively related to both persistence and degree completion among three national samples of Latina/o students" (p. 10).

*College Cocurricular Engagement.* Research on the impact of cocurricular engagement of Latino/as, and Latino males in particular, reports differing results (Baker, 2008; Hurtado & Carter, 1997, Hurtado & Ponjuan, 2005; Kuh, Kinzie, Schuh, & Whitt, 2010; Nuñez, 2009). And there is clearly a need to further explore how active participation in cocurricular activities influences Latino males from different ethnic subgroups.

Kuh et al. (2010) reported that students' campus engagement is a major factor associated with students' college persistence and degree completion. Some research finds that Latino/a students who are actively and consistently engaged in cocurricular activities enhanced their collegiate experiences and increased their commitment to completing a college degree (Hurtado & Carter, 1997; Hurtado & Ponjuan, 2005; Nuñez, 2009). In contrast to Kuh et al.'s (2010) research, however, some scholars found that Latino male engagement in cocurricular activities (for example, social organizations), regardless of their ethnic subgroup, was negatively related to academic outcomes (Baker, 2008).

For some Latino male students, an unwelcoming campus climate has a negative influence on their academic well-being and performance, but these students can develop self-reliant coping skills to navigate a difficult campus climate (Gloria, Castellanos, Scull, & Villegas, 2009). Latino males may also benefit from participation in male-focused student organizations to help improve their college engagement and other outcomes (Saenz & Ponjuan, 2011). Bowman, Park, and Denson (2015) found that participation in racial/ethnic student organizations is positively related to several civic engagement outcomes.

## Recommendations

We must identify the barriers that impede Latino male educational progress and promote promising programs and policies that improve these outcomes for males in all Latino ethnic subgroups. For example, college enrollment is the first step necessary for college credential completion. Institutions need to investigate Latino male college-application patterns with a focus on geographic location. Researchers have found that Hispanic students have different application patterns based on geographic proximity to higher education institutions (Desmond & Turley, 2009). Therefore, 2- and 4-year institutions should adapt their outreach efforts (for example, college fairs, financial aid application seminars, and family college tours) to specific geographic areas and underserved Latino male ethnic subgroups.

Next, institutions need to develop institutional programming focused on Latino male retention—for example, an extended orientation—Latino male "College 101"—developed with Latino males in mind. Such a program can address academic success strategies and personal and practical competency, such as personal finance, accessing campus resources, and improving interpersonal skills. These types of programs may also enhance Latino male students' sense of belonging (Hurtado & Ponjuan, 2005).

Finally, institutions need to increase the recruitment and retention of Latino/a faculty and staff to help Latino males succeed academically. Latino/a faculty and staff presence on campus positively affects student retention and therefore increases degree completion rates for Latinos/as (Oseguera, Locks, & Vega, 2009; Ponjuan, 2011). Having an ethnically diverse Latino/a faculty and staff in both 2- and 4-year institutions could positively affect the collegiate success of Latino male ethnic subgroups.

## Conclusion

There is compelling empirical evidence that ongoing attention and proactive action are needed to help Latino males achieve positive educational outcomes. However, there are challenges that hamper educational leaders and practitioners in their attempt to adequately address this educational goal. As Crisp et al. (2014) state, "Results also highlight the dearth of literature that attempts to understand how the experiences and factors influencing degree outcomes may be similar or different among subgroups of Latina/o students" (p. 15). This chapter highlights a critical need: Higher education institutions must create and support educational policies and programs for an ethnically diverse Latino male student population.

## References

Baker, C. N. (2008). Under-represented college students and extracurricular involvement: The effects of various student organizations on academic performance. *Social Psychology of Education*, *11*(3), 273–298. doi:10.1007/s11218-007-9050-y

Bowman, N. A., Park, J. J., & Denson, N. (2015). Student involvement in ethnic student organizations: Examining civic outcomes 6 years after graduation. *Research in Higher Education*, *56*(2), 127–145. doi:10.1007/s11162-014-9353-8

Buchmann, C., & DiPrete, T. A. (2006). The growing female advantage in college completion: The role of family background and academic achievement. *American Sociological Review*, *71*(4), 515–541. doi:10.1177/000312240607100401

Ceballo, R., Maurizi, L. K., Suarez, G. A., & Aretakis, M. T. (2014). Gift and sacrifice: Parental involvement in Latino adolescents' education. *Cultural Diversity and Ethnic Minority Psychology*, *20*(1), 116–127. doi:10.1037/a0033472

Ceja, M. (2006). Understanding the role of parents and siblings as information sources in the college choice process of Chicana students. *Journal of College Student Development*, *47*(1), 87–104.

Crisp, G., Taggart, A., & Nora, A. (2014). Undergraduate Latina/o students: A systematic review of research identifying factors contributing to academic success outcomes. *Review of Educational Research.* doi:10.3102/0034654314551064

Cunningham, A. F., & Santiago, D. A. (2008). *Student aversion to borrowing: Who borrows and who doesn't.* Washington, DC: Institute for Higher Education Policy.

Desmond, M., & Turley, R. N. L. (2009). The role of familism in explaining the Hispanic-White college application gap. *Social Problems, 56*(2), 311–334. doi:10.1525/sp.2009.56.2.311

Engberg, M. E., & Wolniak, G. C. (2010). Examining the effects of high school contexts on postsecondary enrollment. *Research in Higher Education, 51*(2), 132–153. doi:10.1007/s11162-009-9150-yoo

Fry, R. (2002). *Latinos in higher education: Many enroll, too few graduate.* Washington, DC: Pew Hispanic Center.

Fry, R., & Taylor, P. (2013). *Hispanic high school graduates pass Whites in rate of college enrollment.* Washington, DC: Pew Hispanic Center.

Garcia, L. M., & Bayer, A. E. (2005). Variations between Latino groups in US postsecondary educational attainment. *Research in Higher Education, 46*(5), 511–533. doi:10.1007/s11162-005-3363-5

Gloria, A. M., Castellanos, J., Scull, N. C., & Villegas, F. J. (2009). Psychological coping and well-being of male Latino undergraduates: *Sobreviviendo la universidad. Hispanic Journal of Behavioral Sciences, 31*(3), 317–339. doi:10.1177/0739986309336845

Heckman, S., Lim, H., & Montalto, C. (2014). Factors related to financial stress among college students. *Journal of Financial Therapy, 5*(1), 19–39. doi:10.4148/1944-9771.1063

Horn, L. J., Chen, X., & Chapman, C. (2003). *Getting ready to pay for college: What students and their parents know about the cost of college tuition and what they are doing to find out* (NCES 2003-030). Washington, DC: National Center for Education Statistics, U.S. Department of Education, and Bureau of Justice Statistics, Office of Justice Programs, U.S. Department of Justice. Retrieved from http://nces.ed.gov/pubs2003/2003030.pdf

Hurtado, S., & Carter, D. F. (1997). Effects of college transition and perceptions of the campus racial climate on Latino college students' sense of belonging. *Sociology of Education, 70*(4), 324–345. doi:10.2307/2673270

Hurtado, S., & Ponjuan, L. (2005). Latino educational outcomes and the campus climate. *Journal of Hispanic Higher Education, 4*(3), 235–251.

Ingels, S., & Dalton, B. (2013). *High school longitudinal study of 2009 first follow-up: A first look at fall 2009 ninth-graders in 2012* (NCES 2014-360). Washington, DC: National Center for Education Statistics. Retrieved from http://nces.ed.gov/pubsearch/pubsinfo.asp?pubid=2014360

Jacob, B. A. (2002). Where the boys aren't: Non-cognitive skills, returns to school and the gender gap in higher education. *Economics of Education Review, 21*(6), 589–598. doi:10.1016/S0272-7757(01)00051-6

Kuh, G. D., Kinzie, J., Schuh, J. H., & Whitt, E. J. (2010). *Student success in college: Creating conditions that matter.* San Francisco, CA: Jossey-Bass.

Lopez, E. M. (1995). Challenges and resources of Mexican American students within the family, peer group, and university: Age and gender patterns. *Hispanic Journal of Behavioral Sciences, 17*(4), 499–508. doi:10.1177/07399863950174006

McDonough, P. M., McClafferty, K. A., & Fann, A. (2002, April). *Rural college opportunity: Issues and challenges.* Paper presented at the annual meeting of the American Educational Research Association, New Orleans, LA.

McKinney, L., & Roberts, T. (2012). The role of community college financial aid counselors in helping students understand and utilize financial aid. *Community College Journal of Research and Practice, 36*(10), 761–774. doi:10.1080/10668926.2011.585112

National Center for Education Statistics. (2008). *2007–08 national postsecondary student aid study* (NPSAS:08). Retrieved from http://nces.ed.gov/pubs2009/2009166.pdf

National Center for Education Statistics. (2009). *High school longtitudinal study of 2009 (HSLS:09) first follow up: A first look at fall ninth-graders in 2012.* Retrieved from http://nces.ed.gov/pubs2014/2014360.pdf

Nuñez, A.-M. (2009). Latino students' transitions to college: A social and intercultural capital perspective. *Harvard Educational Review, 79*(1), 22–48.

Nuñez, A.-M., & Crisp, G. (2012). Ethnic diversity and Latino/a college access: A comparison of Mexican American and Puerto Rican beginning college students. *Journal of Diversity in Higher Education, 5*(2), 78–95. doi:10.1037/a0026810

Nuñez, A.-M., & Kim, D. (2012). Building a multicontextual model of Latino college enrollment: Student, school, and state-level effects. *The Review of Higher Education, 35*(2), 237–263. doi:10.1353/rhe.2012.0004

Oseguera, L., Locks, A. M., & Vega, I. I. (2009). Increasing Latina/o students' baccalaureate attainment: A focus on retention. *Journal of Hispanic Higher Education, 8*(1), 23–53.

Perez, P. A., & McDonough, P. M. (2008). Understanding Latina and Latino college choice: A social capital and chain migration analysis. *Journal of Hispanic Higher Education, 7*(3), 249–265.

Pew Hispanic Center. (2009). *Between two worlds: How young Latinos come of age in America.* Washington, DC: Pew Hispanic Center. Retrieved from http://www.pewhispanic.org/2009/12/11/between-two-worlds-how-young-latinos-come-of-age-in-america/

Ponjuan, L. (2011). Recruiting and retaining Latino faculty members: The missing piece to Latino student success. *Thought & Action, 27*, 99–110.

Roderick, M., Coca, V., & Nagaoka, J. (2011). Potholes on the road to college: High school effects in shaping urban students' participation in college application, four-year college enrollment, and college match. *Sociology of Education, 84*(3), 178–211. doi:10.1177/0038040711411280

Saenz, V. B., & Ponjuan, L. (2009). The vanishing Latino male in higher education. *Journal of Hispanic Higher Education, 8*(1), 54–89.

Saenz, V. B., & Ponjuan, L. (2011). *Men of color: Ensuring the academic success of Latino males in higher education.* Washington, DC: Institute for Higher Education Policy. Retrieved from http://eric.ed.gov/?id=ED527060

Seidel, A. (2014, August 11). When applying for federal aid, "cross your fingers and hope." *National Public Radio* (nprEd). Retrieved from http://www.npr.org/blogs/ed/2014/08/11/336043033/when-applying-for-federal-aid-cross-your-fingers-and-hope

Starobin, S. S., Hagedorn, L. S., Purnamasari, A., & Chen, Y. (2013). Examining financial literacy among transfer and nontransfer students: Predicting financial well-being and academic success at a four-year university. *Community College Journal of Research and Practice, 37*(3), 216–225. doi:10.1080/10668926.2013.740388

Turcios-Cotto, V. Y., & Milan, S. (2013). Racial/ethnic differences in the educational expectations of adolescents: Does pursuing higher education mean something different to Latino students compared to White and Black students? *Journal of Youth and Adolescence, 42*(9), 1399–1412. doi:10.1007/s10964-012-9845-9

U.S. Census Bureau. (2000). *Current population survey: 2000.* Retrieved from http://www.census.gov/hhes/socdemo/education/data/cps/2000/tables.html

U.S. Census Bureau. (2004). *The Hispanic population in the United States: 2004.* Retrieved from http://www.census.gov/population/hispanic/data/2004.html

U.S. Census Bureau. (2005). *Current population survey: 2005.* Retrieved from http://www.census.gov/hhes/socdemo/education/data/cps/2005/tables.html

U.S. Census Bureau. (2007). *The Hispanic population in the United States: 2007.* Retrieved from http://www.census.gov/population/hispanic/data/2007.html

U.S. Census Bureau. (2010). *Current population survey: 2010.* Retrieved from http://www.census.gov/hhes/socdemo/education/data/cps/2010/tables.html

U.S. Census Bureau. (2012a). *Current population survey: 2012*. Retrieved from http://www.census.gov/hhes/socdemo/education/data/cps/2012/tables.html

U.S. Census Bureau. (2012b). *The Hispanic population in the United States: 2012*. Retrieved from http://www.census.gov/population/hispanic/data/2007.html

U.S. Census Bureau. (2013a). *Educational attainment in the United States: 2012*. Retrieved from http://www.census.gov/hhes/socdemo/education/data/cps/2012/tables.html

U.S. Census Bureau. (2013b). *Table 11. Educational attainment of the population 25 years and over by sex and Hispanic origin type: 2012*. Retrieved from http://www.census.gov/population/hispanic/data/2012.html

U.S. Census Bureau. (2013c). *Table 302.60. Percentage of 18-24 year olds enrolled in degree granting institutions, by level of institution and sex and race/ethnicity of student: 1967 through 2012*. Retrieved from http://nces.ed.gov/programs/digest/d13/tables/dt13_302.60.asp

LUIS PONJUAN *is an associate professor in the College of Education and Human Development at Texas A&M University.*

LETICIA PALOMIN *is a doctoral student in the College of Education and Human Development at Texas A&M University.*

ANGELA CALISE *is a master's student in the College of Education and Human Development at Texas A&M University.*

## Lesson Learned #1: Organizational Culture and Leadership Matter

"Culture eats strategy for breakfast" is a common statement made at the on-set of many organizational improvement efforts. Unfortunately, awareness of the power of culture on organizational change does not often translate into actions that successfully overcome an existing organizational culture that is cautious, pessimistic, and distrustful of new change efforts (Kotter, 2012). ATD colleges absent a strong presidential message of commitment to organizational change—in this case increasing student success—never acquired momentum. As a consequence, the change effort was lost before it began (Rutschow et al., 2011). Often these presidents were overly concerned about the potential negative reactions of faculty to an organizational change effort and consequently deferred to the faculty as to whether the effort was warranted.

Conversely, a few ATD colleges began their work with an established culture of innovation and change. They had presidents who were attentive to an institutional identity of being at the forefront of trends in higher education and consistently sought recognition for being among the best colleges in the nation or the state. When ATD was launched at such institutions, it was viewed as an opportunity to stay ahead of the pack and gain additional notoriety (Rutschow et al., 2011). Although important, leadership alone was not sufficient to sustain a college-wide effort to increase student success. Data were also critical.

## Lesson Learned #2: Data Matter

Colleges that initiated broad-scale efforts to increase student success quickly learned about being data rich and information poor. Colleges routinely collect large amounts of student record data. They house data on enrollment, persistence, course registration, retention, completion, grades, grade point average, placement in developmental education, units completed, financial aid, academic probation, degree and certificate completion, and transfer rates—all with the capacity to disaggregate by race, ethnicity, gender, age, income, hours worked per week, and numerous other variables. Unfortunately, in the early stages of Achieving the Dream, colleges rarely transformed their data into meaningful information that could be used to shape change efforts to increase student success. For example, faculty members often were unaware of important student success indicators, such as degree and certificate completion rates, persistence rates, or course completion rates in developmental education. Knowledge of the gaps in success rates among racial and ethnic groups also was absent (Mayer et al., 2014; Rutschow et al., 2011).

It is important to note that, over time, many ATD colleges increased their capacity to collect and use data as part of their institutional effort to increase student success. They learned the value of not only summarizing data, but also communicating data findings with effective graphical displays. Many colleges developed or purchased graphical data dashboards that faculty and staff could quickly access and navigate. Colleges were able to target specific student populations with greater confidence than ever before. The level of sophistication related to the use of data to increase student success was notably higher for many ATD colleges after several years (Mayer et al., 2014; Rutschow et al., 2011). However, colleges discovered that they needed to address other factors to achieve noticeable increases in college student success rates.

## Lesson Learned #3: Scale Matters

Soon after engaging in Achieving the Dream, colleges learned that they needed to divorce themselves from a "boutique" culture of programmatic efforts to increase student success. For decades, they, like many other colleges, designed, implemented, and sustained unique programs to support and increase student success. Often, the success rate of students participating in such programs was higher than the average success rate of the total student population. Unfortunately, the number of students served by these programs was too small to have any significant impact on a college's overall student success rate (González, 2012; Mayer et al., 2014). This does not mean that institutions should not target a group of students who consistently demonstrate less success than other students. It does mean that a program designed to address the success rates of a particular student group must have a plan to serve *all* of the students in that group, and not simply a fraction of the group. Put differently, if a college serves a Latino/a student population of 8,000 students, a program that serves 80 Latino/a students is insufficient.

Moving forward, institutions must be mindful of scale of any effort to increase student success. For each proposed student success program, a college must include a "scale-up" plan. A sufficient plan includes (a) outcome achievement levels that would trigger a decision to scale-up an intervention; (b) budget planning, including additional personnel and operating costs, that would support the scale-up of an intervention; and (c) professional development planning and training that would ensure an effective intervention at scale (González, 2012).

## Lesson Learned #4: Faculty Engagement Matters

Colleges involved in student success efforts learned that faculty engagement mattered. Engagement of the faculty needed to be early, broad, and deep. It involved effective communication, planning, and, in many cases, compensation.

New Directions for Higher Education • DOI: 10.1002/he

It was important to make clear that this was not an effort to identify and replace faculty members who taught courses with low pass rates, a common misconception of faculty members and often used as a countermessage to impede the organizational change effort. It also was important to establish that the effort was not about lowering academic standards or "watering down" the curriculum, another common counter-message used by some to thwart change (Rutschow et al., 2011).

Institutions that achieved effective engagement of faculty emphasized that the role of faculty in their student success efforts was essential. In fact, the most effective ATD colleges developed a "bottom-up" message that their student success effort was faculty driven (Mayer et al., 2014). In these colleges, it was not uncommon to find strong and well-respected faculty members serving as chairs for key student success committees or leadership teams.

The time and effort associated with strong faculty engagement was well planned, with consideration of additional compensation or release time. Administrators and faculty worked collaboratively to develop clear expectations about the role, influence, and accountability of faculty in the college's student success efforts. Release time or other compensation often was provided, given the additional work required of faculty. However, accountability measures also were in place and aligned with targeted student success goals (Mayer et al., 2014).

Lack of faculty engagement was the common attribute of those institutions that did not produce any increased student success. Colleges that faltered also noted that faculty engagement was limited to instructors in developmental education. They observed faculty resistance to engagement because of the time demands associated with new expectations for accreditation, specifically the documentation and use of student learning outcomes. Finally, institutions that faltered noted that most of their faculty never acquired the disposition to use student success outcome data, one of the major tenets of Achieving the Dream (Mayer et al., 2014).

## Lesson Learned #5: Evaluation Matters

Evaluation proved to be another major challenge for most ATD colleges. This was a result of several factors. Most institutional research offices did not routinely design and conduct evaluation studies, especially formative evaluations. The bulk of their time was spent producing compliance reports for state and federal agencies, as well as other outside organizations. Faculty members, too, lacked the capacity and experience of conducting comprehensive evaluations. Most colleges did not offer any training to faculty on conducting program evaluations.

A few ATD colleges now serve as good models for data use and effective evaluation. They share the following characteristics: (a) their institutional research (IR) offices are sufficiently staffed to handle the increase in demand for data and evaluation of student success projects; (b) IR staff are able to transform large amounts of data into meaningful information that informs the progress and impact of student success projects; (c) they can facilitate discussions about the use and relevance of evaluation data; (d) IR staff are strong enough to confront decisions that are not rooted in quality data; and (e) faculty and staff acquired an understanding of the role of data and the process of evaluation. In short, the most effective Achieving the Dream colleges had a sufficient number of individuals who understood, and could act upon, the interdependence of data and leadership.

## Final Thought

In closing, there is a steep learning curve before we achieve sufficient gains in student success rates, especially for students of color and low-income students. The gaps are wide and multiple. Perhaps it is time to separate those who *have the will* and *know the way* to increase student success from those who do not. It is time to not simply try, but also to achieve.

## References

American Association of Community Colleges. (2013). *Community college fact sheet.* Retrieved from http://www.aacc.nche.edu/AboutCC/Pages/fastfactsfactsheet.aspx

Attewell, P., Lavin, D., Domina, T., & Levey, T. (2006). New evidence on college reme-diation. *Journal of Higher Education, 77,* 886–924.

Bailey, M., & Dynarski, S. (2011). Inequality in postsecondary attainment. In G. Duncan & R. Murnane (Eds.), *Whither opportunity: Rising inequality, schools, and children's life chances* (pp. 117–132). New York, NY: Russell Sage Foundation.

Bailey, T., Jeong, D. W., & Cho, S. W. (2010). Referral, enrollment, and completion in developmental education sequences in community colleges. *Economics of Education Review, 29,* 255–270.

Belfield, C., Crosta, P., & Jenkins, D. (2014). Can community colleges af-ford to improve completion? *Educational Evaluation and Policy Analysis.* doi:10.3102/0162373713517293

Bernal, D. D. (2002). Critical race theory, Latino critical theory, and critical raced-gendered epistemologies: Recognizing students of color as holders and creators of knowledge. *Qualitative Inquiry, 8,* 105–126.

Bok, D. (2004). *Universities in the marketplace: The commercialization of higher education.* Princeton, NJ: Princeton University Press.

Bok, D. (2013). *Higher education in America.* Princeton, NJ: Princeton University Press.

Bowen, W. G., & Bok, D. (2000). *The shape of the river: The long-term consequences of con-sidering race in college and university admissions.* Princeton, NJ: Princeton University Press.

Campaign for College Opportunity. (2013). *The state of Latinos in higher education in California.* Retrieved from http://collegecampaign.org/portfolio/november-2013 -the-state-of-latinos-in-higher-education-in-california/

CollegeMeasures.org. (2014). *Improving higher education outcomes in the United States.* Retrieved from http://Collegemeasures.org

college choice found that Latino/a students are very responsive to perceptions about price, even if it means passing on one's first-choice institution. The study found that Latino/a students are likely to be more responsive to perceptions about college price and financial aid than most other racial categories, including White and Asian students. Although Kim does not squarely position HSIs against other institutions, his use of the concept of "first choice" versus actual choice has continued to be salient for Latino/a college students. Santiago's (2008a) research on how Latino/as choose colleges helps to provide more detail on the choice patterns between first-choice and actual-choice institutions for this student population. Her study, which included focus groups of Latino/a students who attended and did not attend HSIs, found that, once again, Latino/a students made choices about college attendance related to their perceptions about the availability of financial aid.

The Bill and Melinda Gates Foundation is particularly interested in understanding completion and how financial aid might create more positive results. In 2013, they published a series of papers that sought to understand the college persistence and financial aid challenge from a variety of perspectives. One of these papers is *Using a Latino Lens to Reimagine Aid Design and Delivery* (Santiago, 2013). The paper relies on a combination of statistics and case studies to make the case for four key considerations that frame the entire series on reimagining student aid design and delivery. These considerations include:

1. Considering how financial aid design and implementations might serve non-"traditional" students
2. Developing policies that favor access and completion for low-income students
3. Including student support services
4. Assuring strategic outreach to the community.

In her paper, Santiago (2013) suggests a "posttraditional" view of the Latino/a student population. She dispels myths about Latino/as' preparation for postsecondary work. Using U.S. Census Bureau data, she shows that the majority of Latino/as in K–20 education are native born, speak English fluently, and have families that value education. She reminds policy makers that although a large number of Latino/a students follow a traditional path from high school to college, there are still a number of Latino/a students who follow a circuitous route and many of them tend to be older students. A number of case studies are provided through the paper to give context to the experiences of "posttraditional" potential Latino/a college goers. She reminds readers that the majority of Latino/a students in the United States attend Hispanic-serving institutions.

One of the most powerful stories told in the paper (Santiago, 2013) relates challenges with the FAFSA. Although Latino/as tend to complete the

FAFSA in higher numbers than their White and Asian counterparts, they do not receive as much financial aid despite having lower expected family contributions. Some of this can be explained by financial aid policies that skew toward awarding aid based on academic achievement rather than financial need. Additional data provided in the report suggest that Latino/a students, like their low-income peers, tend to work more to pay school and other costs and may be more likely to be part-time students as a result. Financial aid policies that have stringent time-to-degree requirements penalize students who do not fall into a traditional pattern of full-time course taking. The paper concludes with recommendations related to federal Pell grants as entitlements, the return of the summer federal Pell grant, monetary support for remedial education, and a reiteration of the responsibilities of postsecondary institutions, as well as a recommendation for government and local communities to engage "post-traditional" Latino/a students with consistent and correct messages about financial aid opportunities. Malcom, Dowd, and Yu's (2010) paper related to HSI-STEM (science, technology, engineering, mathematics) funding found that students expected to take advantage of a "balanced approach" to financing their postsecondary education. They hoped to include a combination of institutional, governmental, and family support as part of their college-financing plan. Most of the students in this study were considered traditional—they did not fit all of the criteria that Santiago (2013) highlights as "posttraditional." However, they did mirror the "posttraditional" perspectives in that transfer students expected to rely more on their own support prior to moving onto a 4-year institution.

## Research on Institutional Approaches

The initial Title V legislation empowered selected institutions to engage in a range of 14 possible activities that were expected to support better student outcomes through the "Developing HSI" program. After 6 years of funding there was a reduction from 14 to 8 "allowable" activities for HSIs via Title V funding (Villarreal & Santiago, 2012). The change was based on the belief that "streamlining" through better transfer pathways increases the opportunity for students to receive more direct service via Title V funds. One of the revised activities during this legislative revision included support for low-income students in the form of scholarships, fellowships, and other financial assistance. Villarreal and Santiago's analysis of the number of Title V awards shows that even before the revised list of activities was developed, at least 102 of the 370 institutional grantees chose to use their funds for student support activities including counseling (peer, career, personal), tutoring and mentoring, establishing learning communities, improving student facilities and computer labs, improving student retention and graduation rates, and increasing academic achievement.

New Directions for Higher Education • DOI: 10.1002/he

Slovacek, Whittinghill, Flenoury and Wiseman's (2012) study of the programs funded by the National Institute of Health Minority Opportunities in Research and Education (MORE) found that the stipends and fellowships provided to undergraduate students doing research in the health sciences were essential to the students' persistence in their degree programs and in the field. Financial support was noted as one piece of the success of the program—faculty mentoring and academic preparation were also highlighted as a key parts of the program design. Aligned resources for students are mentioned equally in other work as well (Chase, Bensimon, Shieh, Jones, & Dowd, 2013; Núñez & Bowers, 2011).

In *Reality Check: Hispanic Serving Institutions on the Texas Border Strategizing Financial Aid*, Santiago (2010) describes the collaboration of an entire system of 2- and 4-year colleges on the Texas border. She identifies a number of services, including financial aid support, as key aspects of the programs and services that make up this regional consortium. The patterns of services described in the report are echoed in an even broader investigation of campus practices for Latino/a students at HSIs (Santiago, 2008b). This analysis of 12 institutions across the United States found that successful interventions for this student population included a mix of academic support, community outreach, faculty action, a clear and sustained transfer pathways, and authentic community engagement (Santiago, 2008b). Santiago does not mention financial aid as a key recommendation within this particular paper. However, a closer look at the examples and vignettes presented suggest that financial support was a key element in effective programs. Another study of emerging HSIs (Santiago, 2010) makes the case for developing programming through systematic marketing and enrollment strategies that accurately and clearly communicate financial aid options to potential students. This paper acknowledges the reality that Latino/a students and families may be reluctant or unable to conceptualize different financing options and recommends that accurate financial aid discussions be a significant part of student support services for emerging HSIs.

## Analysis and Conclusion

The main research question that guided this review of the literature is: What does the research tell us about how HSIs organize themselves to support financial aid for Latino/a students? Based on the data presented here, HSIs are no further behind or ahead of other institutions in addressing the financial aid needs of their student populations. The challenges outlined by the scholars identified in this literature review are aligned. Latino/a students make decisions about what colleges to attend based on financial aid choices, which, as Looney (2011) and others found, helps to explain the natural emergence of HSIs in areas of the country with high populations of Latino/as. A review of the articles and papers considered here suggests that there is considerable alignment between the kinds of interventions that are used by HSIs to support Latino/a student populations. It could be argued that much of this alignment is driven by federal legislation. However, Villarreal and Santiago's (2012) analysis of selected activities by emerging HSIs shows that these institutions were making specific choices to engage in some interventions, such as additional student support services, and were not choosing to participate in others—i.e., increasing endowment funds. The most popular interventions included additional student support services, faculty and peer mentoring and/or engagement activities, and curricular streamlining (i.e., developing transfer pathways). What is missing is the strategic planning and coordination of financial aid services with other student programming. A recent analysis of federal policy in relation to Latino/a student success argued that changes in the U.S. population, national college completion goals, and the continuing growth of HSIs—in addition to other minority-serving institutions—necessitate attention to the ways that Latino/a students are able to finance, access, and complete postsecondary education (Santiago, Kienzl, Sponsler, & Bowles, 2010). Financial aid is important to all students, but this review presents evidence that suggest financial aid and perceptions about aid are especially notable for Latino/a students—whether they fit into a traditional or posttraditional category.

HSIs are doing the right thing when they intentionally align support services for students, but they could be doing even better if they intentionally worked to align financial aid policy to connect to institutional or completion goals. External pressures from the federal government and the general public are driving these demands. There are state and federal limitations at play, but public and private institutions can find ways to help Latino/a students gain more consistent benefits from financial aid and related resources.

## Note

1. Hispanic and Latino/a are used interchangeably in this chapter. Hispanic is the federally used term, whereas Hispanic and Latino/a are used in related writing and literature informing this chapter.

## References

Chase, M. M., Bensimon, E. M., Shieh, L. T., Jones, T., & Dowd, A. C. (2013). Constraints and opportunities for practitioner agency in STEM programs in Hispanic serving community colleges. In R. T. Palmer & J. L. Wood (Eds.), *Community colleges and STEM: Examining underrepresented racial and ethnic minorities* (pp. 172–192). New York, NY: Routledge.

Fletcher, C. (2010). *Profile of minority serving institutions in Texas: A study of historically Black colleges and universities and Hispanic serving institutions.* Austin, TX: Texas Guaranteed.

Galvan, J. L. (2009). *Writing literature reviews* (4th ed.). Los Angeles, CA: Pyrczak Publishing.

NEW DIRECTIONS FOR HIGHER EDUCATION • DOI: 10.1002/he

Gross, J. P., Torres, V., & Zerquera, D. (2013). Financial aid and attainment among students in a state with changing demographics. *Research in Higher Education, 54*(4), 383–406.

Kim, D. (2004). The effect of financial aid on students' college choice: Differences by racial groups. *Research in Higher Education, 45*(1), 43–70.

Lee, J. M. (2013). *Inside APLU: Committed to supporting Hispanic-serving institutions.* Washington, DC: Association of Public and Land Grant Universities. Retrieved from http://www.pressreleasepoint.com/inside-aplu-committed-supporting-hispanic-serving-institutions

Looney, S. M. (2011). *Financial literacy at minority serving institutions.* Washington, DC: Institute for Higher Education Policy. Retrieved from http://files.eric.ed.gov/fulltext/ED527709.pdf

Malcom, L. E., Dowd, A. C., & Yu, T. (2010). *Tapping HSI-STEM funds to improve the Latina and Latino access to STEM professions.* Los Angeles, CA: University of Southern California.

McBain, L. (2011). *State need-based and merit-based grant aid: Structural intersections and recent trends.* Washington, DC: American Association of State Colleges and Universities. Retrieved from http://www.aascu.org/uploadedFiles/AASCU/Content/Root/PolicyAndAdvocacy/PolicyPublications/State%20Need-Based%20and%20Merit-Based%20Grant%20Aid.pdf

National Center for Education Statistics. (2011). *Digest of education statistics* (Table 209). Washington, DC: U.S. Department of Education. Retrieved from http://nces.ed.gov/programs/digest/d11/tables/dt11_209.asp

National Center for Education Statistics. (2014). *Digest of education statistics* (Table 306.10). Washington, DC: U.S. Department of Education. Retrieved from http://nces.ed.gov/programs/digest/d14/tables/dt14_306.10.asp?current=yes

National Conference of State Legislatures. (n.d.). *Undocumented student tuition: State action.* Retrieved from http://www.ncsl.org/research/education/undocumented-student-tuition-state-action.aspx#2

Núñez, A. M., & Bowers, A. J. (2011). Exploring what leads high school students to enroll in Hispanic-serving institutions: A multilevel analysis. *American Educational Research Journal, 48*(6), 1286–1313.

Santiago, D. A. (2008a). *Choosing Hispanic-serving institutions (HSIs): A closer look at Latino/a students' college choices.* Washington, DC: Excelencia in Education.

Santiago, D. A. (2008b). *Modeling Hispanic-serving institutions (HSIs): Campus practices that work for Latino/a students.* Washington, DC: Excelencia in Education.

Santiago, D. A. (2010). *Reality check: Hispanic-serving institutions on the Texas border: Strategizing financial aid.* Washington, DC: Excelencia in Education.

Santiago, D. A. (2013). *Using a Latino lens to reimagine aid design and delivery.* Washington, DC: Excelencia in Education.

Santiago, D. A., Kienzl, G. S., Sponsler, B. A., & Bowles, A. (2010). *Ensuring America's future: Federal policy and Latino/a college completion.* Washington, DC: Excelencia in Education.

Slovacek, S., Whittinghill, J., Flenoury, L., & Wiseman, D. (2012). Promoting minority success in the sciences: The minority opportunities in research programs at CSULA. *Journal of Research in Science Teaching, 49,* 199–217.

St. John, E. P. (1992). Workable models for institutional research on the impact of student financial aid. *Journal of Student Financial Aid, 22*(3), 13–26.

St. John, E. P., Cabrera, A. F., Nora, A., & Asker, E. H. (2000). Economic influences on persistence reconsidered: How can finance research inform the reconceptualization of persistence models? In J. Braxton (Ed.), *Reworking the student departure puzzle* (pp. 29–47). Nashville, TN: Vanderbilt University Press.

Villarreal, R. C., & Santiago, D. A. (2012). *From capacity to success: Hispanic-serving institutions (HSIs) and Latino/a student success through Title V.* Washington, DC: Excelencia in Education.

Zarate, M. E., & Burciaga, R. (2010). Latinos and college access: Trends and future directions. *Journal of College Admission, 209,* 24–29.

KRISTAN M. VENEGAS *is a professor of clinical education and research associate in the Pullias Center for Higher Education in the Rossier School of Education at the University of Southern California.*

NEW DIRECTIONS FOR HIGHER EDUCATION • DOI: 10.1002/he

9

This chapter examines the importance of culturally relevant imagery and representation and identity development curriculum for college students. It calls for higher education institutions to embrace cultural strengths as an asset rather than a deficit.

# Lucha Libre and Cultural Icons: Identity Formation for Student Success at HSIs

## Nicholas D. Natividad

In *Deschooling Society*, Ivan Illich (1971) discussed an unalterable framework within the schooling system. He called this framework schooling's hidden curriculum. Noting that in order to understand the hidden curriculum one must first separate learning from schooling, Illich asserted that we must begin to discern between the humanistic goals of the teacher to promote student learning from the impact of the invariant structure of schooling, which limits learning. The structure of schooling, according to Illich, is more concerned with the education that an individual consumes rather than with the learning that is taking place. In other words, "the more education an individual consumes, the more 'knowledge stock' he acquires and the higher he rises in the hierarchy of knowledge capitalists" (Illich, 1978, p. 71). As a result, education defines a new class structure for society, differentiating between those who have greater quantities of knowledge stock and those who do not. Those who have greater quantities of knowledge "can claim to be of superior value to society" (p. 72). According to Illich, "the hidden curriculum thus both defines and measures what education is, and to what level of productivity it entitles the consumer" (p. 72).

It is important for us to understand the hidden curriculum described by Illich (1978) and how it relates to the goal of Hispanic-serving institutions (HSIs) as spaces/distinctions of enterprises for education consumers within the hierarchy of knowledge capitalism versus spaces of learning that contribute to identity formation that, in turn, results in the development of communities. It is the same distinction that many scholars have articulated as the difference between Hispanic-*enrolling* schools versus Hispanic-*serving* schools (Gasman, 2008). Hispanic-*enrolling* schools only facilitate the hierarchy of knowledge capitalism whereas Hispanic-*serving* schools create spaces of learning that interweave culture and identity. These

NEW DIRECTIONS FOR HIGHER EDUCATION, no. 172, Winter 2015 © 2015 Wiley Periodicals, Inc.
Published online in Wiley Online Library (wileyonlinelibrary.com) • DOI: 10.1002/he.20156

distinctions are crucial because many studies focus on the issues of Latino/a students and their difficulties making the transition into higher education. This chapter asserts that transition difficulties for students of color, particularly Latino/as, stem from the processes of schooling that leave many wondering what education is for.

This chapter explores two strategies that contribute to Latino/a student success in HSIs. The first is imagery and representation in recruitment. I discuss how attaching cultural icons to college-going messages cognitively remaps who is allowed to attend college and who is allowed to be successful in college. The second is the importance of a curriculum of identity development in higher education—a curriculum that combats Illich's (1978) hidden curriculum of schooling. Both strategies address the most apparent disconnection of education from the lives of Latino/a students—how culture is not part of the knowledge stock that is built into the hierarchy of education in colleges and universities today. This chapter asserts that Latino/a students have difficulties making the transition into higher education because of the predominant framework of higher education, described by Illich, which creates education consumers within a hierarchy of knowledge capitalism. Instead, this chapter calls for the examination of how culture is always considered separate and does not contribute to the knowledge stock that individuals can claim as valuable to themselves and for society. This includes the examination of hidden curriculum to understand what lies beneath the structure of schooling that is disallowing Latino/a students to make a successful transition into higher education.

## Imagery and Representation

How well Latino/a students do in school is often influenced by larger identities in society. Critical educational theorists have debated how schools help to transmit societal status and class positions (McLaren, 2009). This debate has included understanding the complexities of the relationship between schools and dominant society. In addition, it also includes what resistance theorists like Henry Giroux (Giroux, 1981; Giroux & Robbins, 2006) have revealed—that the school system reflects and sustains dominant social practices and structures that are found in larger class-, race-, and gender-divided society (McLaren, 1994, 2009). When viewing the schooling process we find the treatment of race-based populations to be based on stereotypes and biased assumptions, and often the schooling process contributes to and reinforces these biases. To what extent do processes found in schooling reflect dominant social practices and structures when looking at the larger society's perceptions of Latino/as and the subsequent recruitment practices of higher education institutions that result from these perceptions?

Hayes-Bautista (2004) discussed how non-Hispanic Whites perceive people of Mexican origin. In a focus group, he examined the opinions of

White subjects about a television commercial that depicted Latino/as in a variety of professional positions. The commercial was meant to depict Latino/as as quintessential Americans with advanced degrees (medical researcher, businessman, college graduates) living out the American dream. However, when asked about their opinion of the commercial, the White subjects had a difficult time perceiving Latino/as in these positions and, in particular, of seeing Latino/as as striving to achieve the American dream. He noted that the "key element of the American dream was the desire to achieve more, to accomplish more, to better oneself, [and] they were not sure that Latinos really wanted to progress, particularly into the middle class" (Hayes-Bautista, 2004, p. 163).

The result of this perception and dominant perceptions in society take a detrimental toll on Latino/a students. As Gándara and Contreras (2009) explained,

> This is the perception against which Latino youth must attempt to construct an identity as a good student and an aspirant into the American middle-class. For many Latino students, the struggle to reconcile the perceptions of others will result in their rejecting either their ethnicity or the role of good student, neither of which augurs well for healthy personal or psychological development. (p. 79)

These perceptions are crucial to understanding recruiting practices of higher education institutions. How do higher education institutions combat dominant perceptions while at the same time honor and facilitate the strengthening of an entering student's ethnicity?

Duncan-Andrade and Morrell (2008) provided a case study that sheds light on creating a liberating language and message. The South City High School Futures Project used critical pedagogy to develop a collective language among students that allowed them to make sense of the realities associated with attending high school. This collective language allowed for an empowering critique of the conditions the students faced and illuminated alternative pathways and identities with which they could associate in order to engage the school without losing their agency or cultural identity. This project is significant because by developing this collective language of critique, the students were able to confront the school and navigate it within an understanding of their own reality. Using their own language allowed them to convey and discover their own alternative pathways. Instead of simply allowing students to turn away from the school, the critical-pedagogy educators provided them with tools that justified and embraced their own realities, allowing them to confront the school structure and navigate it on their own terms with their own alternative pathways.

Often higher education institutions produce cookie-cutter platforms and pathways of recruitment and outreach services for students, yet fail to engage students within their own realities. As a result, these institutions do not provide different ways of understanding higher education to allow students to discover a "collective language" that makes sense of their world and connects their realities to higher education goals and purposes (Duncan-Andrade & Morrell, 2008). Without this collective language new pathways cannot be achieved. Latino/as are diverse populations with even more diverse communities stretched out across the United States. A recruitment strategy that works well in one community may not work in other communities. The key to understanding what does and does not work is found in Duncan-Andrade and Morrell's approach, which is finding the collective language that is born out of a "critique"—a critical examination of the schooling processes that contribute and reinforce stereotypes and biases and result in the disconnect between campus culture and students' home culture.

Therefore, a starting point for higher education leaders will be to ask what their colleges and/or universities are not doing for Latino/a students in their region and the specific communities they are trying to serve. In other words, each institution has to engage in a critique in order to bridge existing gaps and serve student needs and realities.

One example of critiquing the institution is found in the Nepantla Program at Nevada State College. The term "Nepantla" is a Nahuatl (Aztec language) term connoting "in-between" or a reference to the space of "the middle" or "torn between worlds." Several artists, poets, and scholars have used this term and its symbolism in their work, enriching and adding to the concept (Anzaldua, 1987; Mora, 1993; Venegas, 2007). The larger cultural space of Nepantla has become a postmodern paradigm or consciousness rooted in the creation of a "new middle" (Venegas, 2007). The academic faculty and founders of the program at Nevada State College use the term Nepantla to connote the space in which many first-generation and underrepresented college students find themselves, being "torn between worlds" or "in between" social locations. The symbolism behind the term is part of the founders' attempt to foster a collective language with Latino/a students by noting the transitions that many students face in the high school to college transition. The Nepantla Program mixes imagery and representation of cultural icons and terminology to connect to the students within their own lived realities. This helps students carve out a space in higher education where they can manifest their identities and beliefs in culture and education and allow for the creation of a "new middle" using cultural strengths as an asset rather than a deficit. The three posters in Figure 9.1 demonstrate the collective message of who belongs in college and sets the tone for recruitment strategies developed by the founders of the program and employed by higher education institutions.

By using symbolism, imagery, and representation in recruitment, the Nepantla Program is an alternative space carved out for students that reinterprets and redefines the role of college recruitment by attaching a

NEW DIRECTIONS FOR HIGHER EDUCATION • DOI: 10.1002/he

### Figure 9.1. Nepantla Program Posters

college-going message to a culture that is not often associated with college. As Cesaretti (1975) explained,

> A Chicano kid grows up with walls of many kinds around him. When somebody is born into that situation, there are several things he can do. He can ignore the walls and sink into apathy or he can become violent and try to blow up the walls. But there is a third way, a way that people have used for centuries. And that is to perform a kind of ritual magic to neutralize the force of the walls by decorating them with signs, symbols and art. Chicano street writers choose this third way. (p. 23)

Imagery and representation have the ability to break down walls of dominant stereotypes and social perceptions and, more importantly, to develop a collective language and message among higher education

**Figure 9.1.** (*Continued*)

institutions and the populations they serve. College and universities use imagery and representation featuring dominant social practices that are accepted and exalted. How buildings are named, statues erected, painting and murals displayed, and even how spaces are designed on campus reflect the dominant campus narrative. The first step for any institution trying to engage in the critique from the perspective of the students they serve is to build a collective language, message, and environment that integrate cultural icons, practices, and realities of the students. By doing so, higher education institutions will begin to go beyond rhetoric and embrace cultural difference as a place of knowledge and power. This, in turn, creates an environment conducive to developing a curriculum of identity development.

## Curriculum of Identity Development

The social identity of Latino/as in the United States has long been plagued by the mark of illegality and perpetual immigration. Chavez (2008) discussed how public discourse in the United States has created and perpetuated the stereotype of Latino/as as the quintessential foreigners or "illegal aliens." He posited that Latinos are not like previous immigrant groups, who ultimately became part of the nation. According to the assumptions and taken-for-granted "truths" inherent in this narrative, Latinos are unwilling or incapable of integrating, of becoming part of the national community. Accordingly, the "Latino threat narrative" creates the assumption that Latino/as are part of an invading force that ultimately destroys the American way of life because of their inability to assimilate. The construction of knowledge around Latino/as as perpetual illegal aliens has a long historical presence in the United States. This narrative has been created, embedded, and reinforced historically through multiple institutions including media, immigration laws, academic scholarship, and government policies. The construction of this knowledge has served to marginalize, impoverish, and disenfranchise Latino/as on social, economic, political, and legal levels. It has resulted in relegating Latino/as to the status of "illegitimate members" of society and thus undeserving of social benefits.

This narrative is important for us to consider when thinking about the social climate Latino/a students encounter in higher education institutions. The question of whether Latino/a students belong in all social settings in America, including college, simmers in the back of many Latino/a students' minds. Because this historical narrative has constructed knowledge about Latino/as, it has created and reinforced processes of objectification that in turn leads to dehumanizing practices toward Latino/as as evidenced in particular legal, economic, and political structures and policies (Chacón & Davis, 2006; Chavez, 2008; López, 2003). This narrative can help us to examine how and where schools—in this context, colleges and universities—perpetuate and reproduce attitudes, stereotypes, and social relationships that contribute to dominant and class relations.

Critical educational theorists view school knowledge as historically and socially rooted and interest bound. In other words, "knowledge acquired in school—or anywhere for that matter—is never neutral or objective but is ordered and structured in particular ways" (McLaren, 2009, p. 63). McLaren goes on to explain that emphases and exclusions in the production of knowledge in school partake of a "silent logic" that justifies dehumanization processes. Silent logic can also be understood as the development of a particular reasoning or hegemony that results from knowledge being reinforced and emphasized in socialization and conditioning process that are part of schooling. (For more information about the concept of silent logic, see http://www.scribd.com/doc/153729927/Sousa-Santos-A-Critique -of-Lazy-Reason#scribd.) So the question is not how do we combat the cultural politics of knowledge production, but rather how do we combat a logic that creates and sustains practices of dehumanization and is reinforced in educational spaces such as colleges and universities?

McLaren (2009) maintained that schooling should be "a process of examining how we have been constructed out of the prevailing ideas, values, and worldviews of the dominant culture" (p. 80): in other words, how schooling should include scrutinizing and critically engaging social constructions of race, gender, sexuality, and other fabricated hierarchies in order to reveal stereotypes and biases and understand how dominant culture produces these constructions. McLaren pointed out that students enter the schooling environment with a constructed social identity. Therefore, the beginning step for any transition program at HSIs should be to embed a curriculum that deconstructs and teaches the complexity of social constructions of identity in order to flip the script on what Claude Steele calls "stereotype threat" (Steele & Aronson, 1995). Once a curriculum allows students to understand how identities are constructed for social agendas, students can then begin to understand how dominant perceptions have been interwoven into their own perceptions of the world and their own identity.

Bourdieu and Passeron (1977) argued that the knowledge of the upper and middle classes is considered valuable capital within a hierarchical society. They maintained that social inequities exist because of the knowledge that is accumulated within middle and upper-class families and is valued by privileged societal groups. They asserted that, as a result, social hierarchical society reproduces itself. What Bourdieu and Passeron illuminated is a significant point for class relations. However, in applying this to race relations in the United States, we see that social hierarchical society reproduces itself not through knowledge accumulated among upper and middle classes but instead through the dominant knowledge about race and racism in the United States. In other words, as López (2000) argues, ideas on the social construction of race and its long historical trajectory in the United States have created a particular consciousness within students as they navigate their realities with this biological myth, yet social reality, called race. The issue is not merely the *valuing* of racial groups over others but the *valuing* of particular social constructions of race over others in colleges and universities. As Bourdieu and Passeron (1977) demonstrated, it is not merely enough for middle and upper classes to accumulate knowledge but that this knowledge is *valued* by privileged groups. Similarly it is important to understand how certain groups *value* knowledge on the idea of race and how circulation and reinforcement (or even exclusion in schools) of this knowledge benefit certain groups.

Yosso (2005) examined the benefits of various forms of cultural capital that students of color bring with them from their homes and communities into the classroom. She discussed how these forms often go unnoticed or are left out of classrooms as valid and legitimate knowledge. She posits a critical-race-theory approach can help educators develop schools that "acknowledge the multiple strengths Communities of Color bring in order to serve a larger purpose of struggle towards social and racial justice" (p. 69). Yosso flips the script by critiquing the assumption that students of color come to the classroom with cultural deficiencies.

The theory of community cultural wealth helps us understand the positive impact a curriculum that incorporates culture as a strength rather than a deficiency can have on a student's educational career. Yet, more often than not, specialized curricula that incorporate cultural values are always left

NEW DIRECTIONS FOR HIGHER EDUCATION • DOI: 10.1002/he

out as invalid or illegitimate knowledge stock for higher education. This begs the question, How can students begin to deconstruct myths on the idea of race while understanding them as social realities, if they are not provided academic and critical-thinking tools? A culturally relevant and identity-formation curriculum allows students to use their own cultural capital to understand dominant stereotypes and threat narratives that are motivated by social agendas and that create disillusionment of students toward higher education. Understanding these dominant social perceptions allows students to create and develop their own counternarrative to assist them in confronting the ways that education institutions reinforce these narratives.

Because students come into the classroom with general cultural background or cultural capital (Bourdieu & Passeron, 1977), it is vital to have a curriculum that engages not only dominant cultural knowledge but also community cultural wealth (Yosso, 2005) from the beginning of their educational careers. Doing so demonstrates to all students that their cultural capital is important and empowering and that it can help them deconstruct social constructions of identity.

Implementing a curriculum that links critical social theory to identity formation for students making the transition into higher education is helpful not only in deconstructing narratives/discourses around identity but also in connecting these discourses to larger processes and projects of objectification and dehumanization. Therefore, it is not only about creating and teaching courses about the history of the idea of race but also about building a curriculum that makes connections between critical pedagogy, racial identity, and academic achievement.

## Conclusion

"I've never met a kid with a dysfunctional relationship to learning. I've met a lot of kids with a dysfunctional relationship to school" (Palos, 2011). A dialectical understanding of schooling permits us to view formal educational spaces as sites of both domination and liberation. Even though critical educational theorists remind us that no curriculum, policy, or program is ideologically or politically innocent, a curriculum that links critical social theory to identity formation is helpful to deconstruct narratives/discourses around identity and connect discourses to larger processes and projects of objectification and dehumanization.

Finally, higher education institutions must combat a socially constructed identity of Latino/a students by contributing to the counternarrative that centers Latino/a cultural icons as sources of strength and knowledge. In other words, we must allow students to confront and navigate college by producing college-going messages that connect to their realities. It is not merely about depicting Latino/as in marketing campaigns as successful professionals but also about depicting cultural icons and attaching them to college-going messages. Diversity initiatives in higher education institutions are often siphoned and isolated into corners of the institutions and are not deeply embedded into their overall vision and mission. Instead diversity centers or, I would argue, inappropriately called multicultural centers, run the risk of being superficial symbols of diversity or even worse catering to the manufactured identities and stereotypes that reflect and reinforce dominant perceptions. These superficial symbols directly influence the question that many students who graduate high school ask, "What is college and who is it for?" By embedding imagery and representation that is specific to the communities that higher education institutions are trying to serve, along with creating curricula of identity development for students, higher education can become more than a hierarchy of knowledge capitalism and instead spaces of learning for the development of communities for Latino/a students.

## References

Anzaldua, G. (1987). *Borderlands/La frontera: The new mestiza* (3rd ed.). San Francisco, CA: Aunt Lute Books.

Bourdieu, P., & Passeron, J. (1977). *Reproduction in education, society, and culture.* London, UK: Sage.

Cesaretti, G. (1975). *Street writers: A guided tour of Chicano graffiti.* Los Angeles, CA: Acrobat Books.

Chacón, J., & Davis, M. (2006). *No one is illegal: Fighting violence and state repression on the U.S.-Mexico border.* Chicago, IL: Haymarket Books.

Chavez, L. (2008). *The Latino threat: Constructing immigrants, citizens, and the nation.* Palo Alto, CA: Stanford University Press.

Duncan-Andrade, J. M., & Morrell, E. (2008). *The art of critical pedagogy: Possibilities for moving from theory to practice in urban schools.* New York, NY: Peter Lang.

Gándara, P. C., & Contreras, F. (2009). *The Latino education crisis: The consequences of failed social policies.* Cambridge, MA: Harvard University Press.

Gasman, M. (2008). *Understanding minority-serving institutions.* Albany: State University of New York Press.

Giroux, H. (1981). *Ideology, culture & the process of schooling.* Philadelphia, PA: Temple University Press.

Giroux, H., & Robbins, C. (2006). *The Giroux reader.* Boulder, CO: Paradigm.

Hayes-Bautista, D. E. (2004). *La nueva California Latinos in the Golden State.* Berkeley: University of California Press.

Illich, I. (1971). *Deschooling society.* New York, NY: Harper & Row.

Illich, I. (1978). *Toward a history of needs.* New York, NY: Pantheon Books.

López, I. (2000). The social construction of race. In R. Delgado & J. Stefancic (Eds.), *Critical race theory: The cutting edge* (2nd ed., pp. 191–203). Philadelphia, PA: Temple University Press.

López, I. (2003). *Racism on trial: The Chicano fight for justice.* Cambridge, MA: Belknap Press of Harvard University Press.

McLaren, P. (1994). *Life in schools: An introduction to critical pedagogy in the foundations of education* (2nd ed.). New York, NY: Longman.

McLaren, P. (2009). Critical pedagogy: A look at major concepts. In A. Darder, M. Baltodano, & R. Torres (Eds.), *The critical pedagogy reader* (2nd ed., pp. 61–83). New York, NY: Routledge.

Mora, P. (1993). *Nepantla: Essays from the land in the middle.* Albuquerque: University of New Mexico Press.

Palos, A. (Director). (2011). *Precious knowledge* [Documentary movie]. United States: Dos Vatos Productions.

Steele, C. M., & Aronson, J. (1995). Stereotype threat and the intellectual test performance of African Americans. *Journal of Personality and Social Psychology, 69*(5), 797–811.

Venegas, S. (2007, January 1). *Nepantla.* Retrieved from http://www.chicanoart.org/nepantla.html

Yosso, T. J. (2005). Whose culture has capital? A critical race theory discussion of community cultural wealth. *Race Ethnicity and Education, 8*(1), 69–91.

*NICHOLAS D. NATIVIDAD is an assistant professor of criminal justice at New Mexico State University and cofounder of the Nepantla Program at Nevada State College.*

NEW DIRECTIONS FOR HIGHER EDUCATION • DOI: 10.1002/he

# 10

*This chapter synthesizes the authors' recommendations for academics and practitioners as colleges and universities prioritize institutional policies and programs to ensure Latino/a student success.*

# Moving Forward: Future Directions for Improving Institutional Support for Latino/a Students

*Caitlin J. Saladino, Magdalena Martinez*

President Obama's "College Completion Agenda" has given higher education institutions an enormous responsibility to educate and facilitate degree attainment for America's future leaders from all races and ethnic groups. This volume has focused on the largest of those groups—Latino/as. The chapter authors provide an understanding of the current higher education landscape as it affects Latino/a populations. Authors focus in particular on Hispanic-serving institutions (HSIs) through case-study analysis and theoretical investigations. Each chapter offers suggestions to improve the overall institutional environment and level of support for Latino/a students. In reading these chapters, four overarching themes emerge.

## Theme #1: Latino/a Culture Matters

Natividad (Chapter 9) presents Yosso's (2005) model for community cultural wealth as a framework to understand the valuable skills Latino/a students bring to the college environment. Rather than viewing their Latino/a cultural values as a detriment to their educational success, Natividad argues institutional practices and programs can align with the unique assets students have to offer. Natividad reminds us that by looking at the college experience through the lens of community cultural wealth, educators can incorporate Latino/a culture as a *strength* rather than a deficiency.

Venegas (Chapter 8) reminds us that culture should also be considered in financial aid policies. Latino/a students typically work to pay for school, so financial aid policies that contain time-to-degree-completion stipulations

NEW DIRECTIONS FOR HIGHER EDUCATION, no. 172, Winter 2015 © 2015 Wiley Periodicals, Inc.
Published online in Wiley Online Library (wileyonlinelibrary.com) • DOI: 10.1002/he.20157

are disadvantageous. Although many colleges and universities engage in cultural interventions through additional support services, few institutions plan their financial aid programs strategically. The limited available scholarship on HSIs and financial aid inhibits practitioners from understanding how cultural practice may conflict with financial access for Latinos/as in higher education.

Kiyama, Museus, and Vega (Chapter 3) present the Culturally Engaging Campus Environments (CECE) framework. They encourage institutions to create environments, using the CECE, where all students can thrive. They note that physical space is key and provides student groups a place to gather to find cultural familiarity on campus. Additionally they suggest campuses can provide intellectual space where Latino/a studies programs are encouraged and supported and culturally relevant knowledge is praised. Ponjuan, Palomin, and Calise (Chapter 6) assert that thoughtful cocurricular engagement can foster self-reliant coping skills, in particular for Latino male students. Absent these coping skills, Latino males are often left to navigate a difficult campus climate on their own; this can lead to college departure or delayed completion. Gildersleeve and Vigil (Chapter 4) note that for undocumented students supportive environments that are timely and culturally relevant foster a sense of belonging and community where students feel safe to communicate their needs and concerns to campus staff.

## Theme #2: Institutional Change Requires Leadership, Understanding, and Action

Martinez (Chapter 2) urges us to consider emerging HSIs and the process of organizational change. She uses Kezar's (2001) organizational theories of change and suggests that emerging HSIs provide researchers and practitioners opportunities to create proactive policies and programs. She highlights how a group of institutions and key actors engaged in a campaign of HSI awareness, understanding, and action. She points to the important role that governance, leadership, and policy played and offers lessons learned for emerging HSI leaders to ensure that all aspects of systemic change are considered.

Gonzalez (Chapter 7) suggests that organizational culture and leadership were key for "Achieving the Dream" (ATD) colleges and their outcomes. This national initiative received substantial philanthropic support and was hailed as a step in the right direction for community colleges. Gonzalez highlights that a strong sense of commitment from college presidents and senior administration was necessary to facilitate ATD college-wide efforts to increase student success. Freeman (Chapter 1) reminds us that the composition of leadership is important when considering HSI initiatives. She argues that institutions must reexamine the demographic makeup of their administrators and faculty. Although Latino/as represent 19% of 2-year college students and 11% of 4-year college students, there are few Latino/a role models; only 5% of institutional administrators and fewer than 4% of faculty are Latino/a. Freeman notes how the Higher Education Administration and Leadership (HEAL) program at Adams State University attempts to correct this discrepancy.

According to Nuñez and Elizondo (2013), institutional faculty, staff, and administrators can give Latino/as students the guidance they need to navigate the unfamiliar territory of college; when a mentor relationship is fostered, these students are more likely to successfully transfer from 2-year institutions toward a baccalaureate degree. If the individuals in higher education leadership roles do not proportionately represent the students they serve, students may feel they are not validated interpersonally or academically (Nuñez & Elizondo, 2013).

Ultimately, to increase the number of Latinos/as in educational leadership positions, more Latinos/as need to obtain master's and doctoral degrees. Ponjuan, Palomin, and Calise (Chapter 6) suggest that recruitment and retention of Latino/a faculty and staff are crucial to the success of Latino male college students. The presence of Latino/a leaders is key because these role models and mentors emulate the power of education for Latino/a students.

## Theme #3: Latino/as' Aspirational Capital Is an Asset for Student Success

Gildersleeve and Vigil (Chapter 4) note that undocumented students in American higher education are disadvantaged because the complicated legal contexts create an additional series of barriers to college degree attainment. However, they also show that undocumented students aspire to achieve a degree, despite the fact that many do not have the financial means to pay for college and their status prevents their access to federal or state financial aid. Gildersleeve and Vigil suggest that administrators have the power to create supportive infrastructures for undocumented students, which can turn the students' aspirational capital into achievement. The International Office at The University of Texas at Austin and the Undocumented Student Program at the University of California–Los Angeles are examples that institutional leaders can model and help students turn their aspirational capital into student success.

Additionally, Aguirre-Covarrubias, Arellano, and Espinoza (Chapter 5) discuss the aspirational capital of Latina graduate engineering students at an HSI. Their research reveals that persistence in a graduate engineering program was most frequently attributed to having a positive attitude and self-confidence. Yosso's (2005) work on aspirational capital suggests that these Latina students are resilient as they face challenging programs with an idea of what the future could hold. To improve their experience on campus, the chapter authors suggest the formation of Latina graduate student peer support and networking opportunities. They also argue that the importance of high-quality advising cannot be overlooked. Aguirre-Covarrubias,

Arellano, and Espinoza found that Latina graduate students reported negative advising experiences as one of the biggest challenges they faced as they worked toward degree completion. The experience of these Latina students is consistent with previous findings, which suggest that "the quality of academic advisement, access to financial aid, and social and cultural issues" (Gard, Paton, & Gosselin, 2012, p. 833) are the most recurrent factors that impede successful transfer and student success.

Gonzalez (Chapter 7) reminds us that college completion for Latinos/as attending community colleges is limited, and an ineffective system of higher education may be at fault. Ultimately, colleges and universities must be aware of the institutional barriers that prevent students from achieving their college and career aspirations. The authors in this volume underscore the importance of evidence on aspirational capital and urge institutions to acknowledge and incorporate Latino/a assets into their programs and policies.

## Theme #4: Moving Forward: Strengthening Institutional Capacity Through Researcher and Practitioner Collaboration

Much like Freeman's experience with Adams State University (Chapter 1), Martinez (Chapter 2) suggests that institutions must build institutional capacity and create internal HSI task forces comprised of faculty, student services professionals, students, and key external allies. To be truly Hispanic *serving*, colleges and universities need to cultivate a campus culture where all constituency groups see the value of Latinos/as in higher education. Above all else, this volume suggests that it is necessary for researchers and practitioners to consider what has been done before, and make improvements where necessary. In this regard, we can consider the example of Adams State's HEAL program. As Freeman notes (Chapter 1), Adams State had no faculty with PhDs in higher education who could help develop the HEAL program. Freeman and campus senior leadership reached out to HSI academics and practitioners across the country.

This tactic serves as a reminder that as we aim to provide more opportunities for Latino/a students, we must continually collaborate with successful postsecondary leaders across the United States. Gonzalez also urges postsecondary leaders to learn from ATD findings and build a culture of evidence and collaboration in order to strengthen institutional capacity to ensure student success and completion. Gildersleeve and Vigil (Chapter 4) remind us that social media can become an invaluable tool for researchers and practitioners to share institutional-level activities to help better serve students, in this case undocumented students. Collectively, the authors agree that good postsecondary practices to strengthen institutional capacity can be replicated and expanded if genuine collaboration is fostered and promoted.

It is clear that in order for the country to achieve its college completion agenda, a focus on Latino/a student success must be at the forefront of any postsecondary efforts. Colleges and universities—whether emerging or existing HSIs—can be merely Hispanic-*enrolling* or truly Hispanic-*serving* institutions. The authors in this volume offer ample evidence and a framework for how these institutions can move forward and truly be Hispanic-serving colleges and universities.

### References

Gard, D. R., Paton, V., & Gosselin, K. (2012). Student perceptions of factors contributing to community-college-to-university transfer success. *Community College Journal of Research and Practice, 36*(11), 833–848.

Kezar, A. (2001). *Understanding and facilitating organizational change in the 21st century: Recent research and conceptualizations* [ASHE-ERIC Higher Education Report, 28(4)]. San Francisco, CA: Jossey-Bass.

Nuñez, A. M., & Elizondo, D. (2013, Spring). Closing the Latino/a transfer gap: Creating pathways to the baccalaureate. *Perspectivas: Issues in Higher Education Policy and Practice, 2,* 1–12.

Yosso, T. J. (2005). Whose culture has capital? A critical race theory discussion of community cultural wealth. *Race, Ethnicity and Education, 8*(1), 69–91.

*CAITLIN J. SALADINO is a PhD student in higher education at the University of Nevada, Las Vegas, and a research assistant with The Lincy Institute, Education Programs at UNLV.*

*MAGDALENA MARTINEZ is the director of education programs at the Lincy Institute and a faculty member at the University of Nevada, Las Vegas.*

# INDEX

**HE 171   Mentoring as Transformative Practice: Supporting Student and Faculty Diversity**

*Caroline S. Turner*
Scholars examining how women and people of color advance in academia invariably cite mentorship as one of the most important factors in facilitating student and faculty success. Contributors to this volume underscore the importance of supporting one another, within and across differences, as critical to the development of a diverse professoriate. This volume of *New Directions for Higher Education* emphasizes and highlights:
- the importance of mentorship;
- policies, processes, and practices that result in successful mentoring relationships;
- real life mentoring experiences to inform students, beginning faculty, and those who would be mentors; and
- evidence for policy makers about what works in the development of supportive and nurturing higher education learning environments.

The guiding principles underlying successful mentorships, interpersonally and programmatically, presented here can have the potential to transform higher education to better serve the needs of all its members. This will be of interest to faculty, administrators, and policy makers who want to create a supportive mentoring environment.
ISBN: 978-1-119-16106-6

**HE 170   Exploring Diversity at Historically Black Colleges and Universities: Implications for Policy and Practice**

*Robert T. Palmer, C. Rob Shorette II, and Marybeth Gasman*
Though scholars have explored various topics related to Historically Black Colleges and Universities (HBCUs), little empirical research has critically examined the increasingly changing racial demography and social diversity of HBCUs and their impact on HBCU stakeholders. Some stakeholders feel that changing racial demographics could change the culture of these institutions. This volume of *New Directions for Higher Education* provides meaningful context and initiates discussion on the increasingly changing diversity of HBCUs. Not only does this volume contribute to this discussion, but it also:
- offers new information that will help HBCUs be more intentional about creating an inclusive campus environment for all enrolled students,
- discusses the experiences of LGBT, Latino/a, and other minority students enrolled at HBCUs, and
- examines myths and historical contexts of HBCUs.

Aside from the practical implications provided herein, the volume also provides salient context for researchers and policymakers interested in the diversification of HBCUs. Given the range and the depth of the issues covered, it is a must read for anyone interested in HBCUs in general and student success within these institutions specifically.
ISBN: 978-1-119-10843-6

**HE 169**  **Enhancing and Expanding Undergraduate Research: A Systems Approach**

*Mitchell Malachowski, Jeffrey M. Osborn, Kerry K. Karukstis, and Elizabeth L. Ambos*

Undergraduate research is a high-impact practice that sparks students' interest in learning and love for the discipline, and it improves retention, student success, graduation rates, and postgraduation achievement. Many individual campuses have offered these programs for several years, and the Council on Undergraduate Research (CUR) has supported their efforts in many ways. More recently, CUR has partnered with state systems of higher education and public and private consortia to foster the institutionalization of undergraduate research at the member institutions and across the systems/consortia.

This volume illustrates many of the successes that entire systems/consortia and their campuses have achieved, such as:

- connecting undergraduate research to the curriculum, student success and completion, especially for underrepresented students,
- creating cross-campus discussions on curricula and pedagogy, research collaborations among departments and campuses, and enhanced interdisciplinary activities, and
- addressing the challenges of workforce development and faculty issues—especially workload and tenure/promotion.

Lessons from building a rich undergraduate research program across the systems can be applied to many other system-wide initiatives. This is of interest to faculty, administrators, and practitioners.

ISBN: 978-1-119-06136-6